Easter

Adult Coloring Book

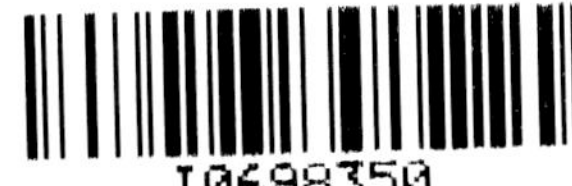

this book belongs to

____

____

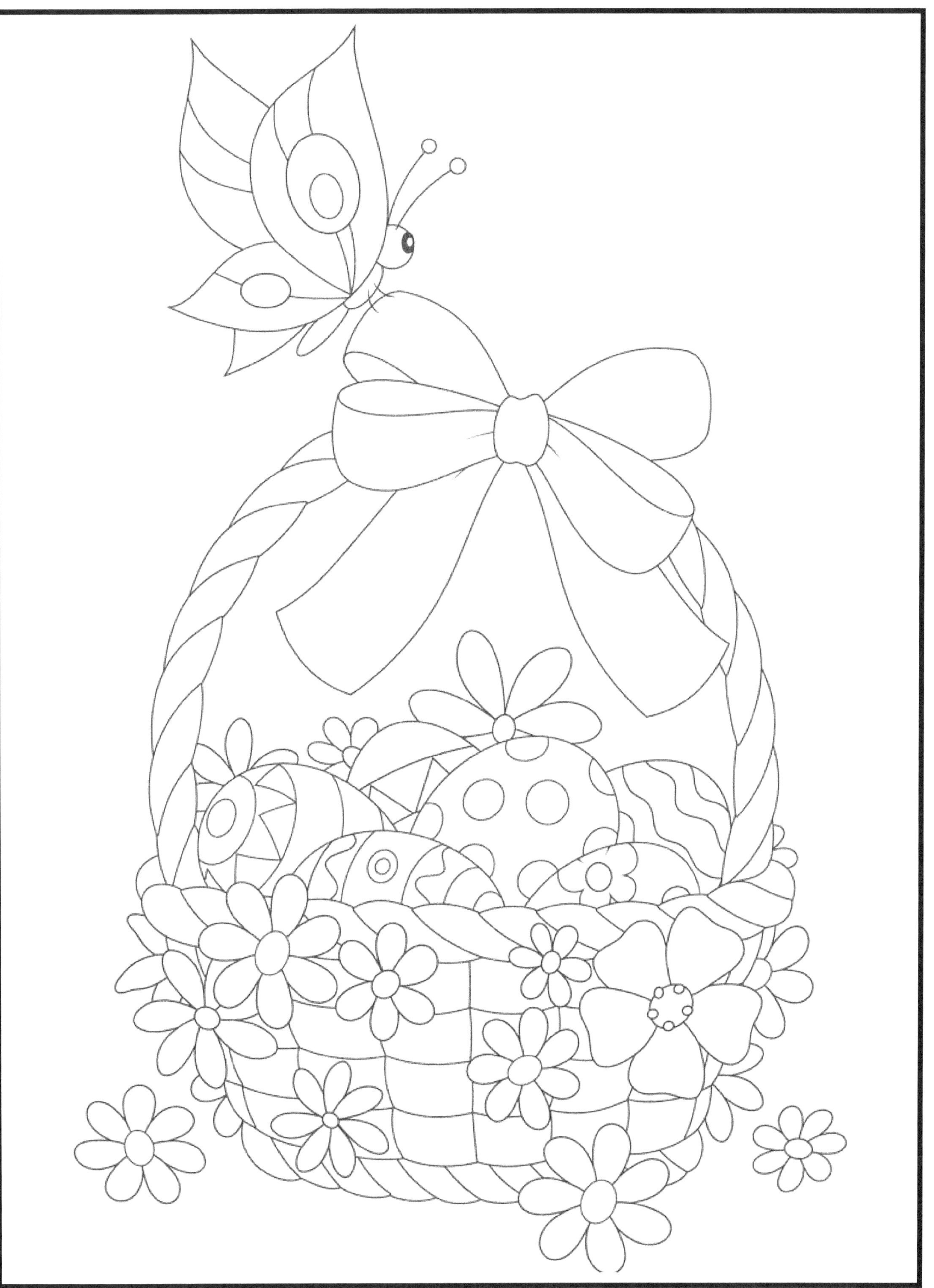

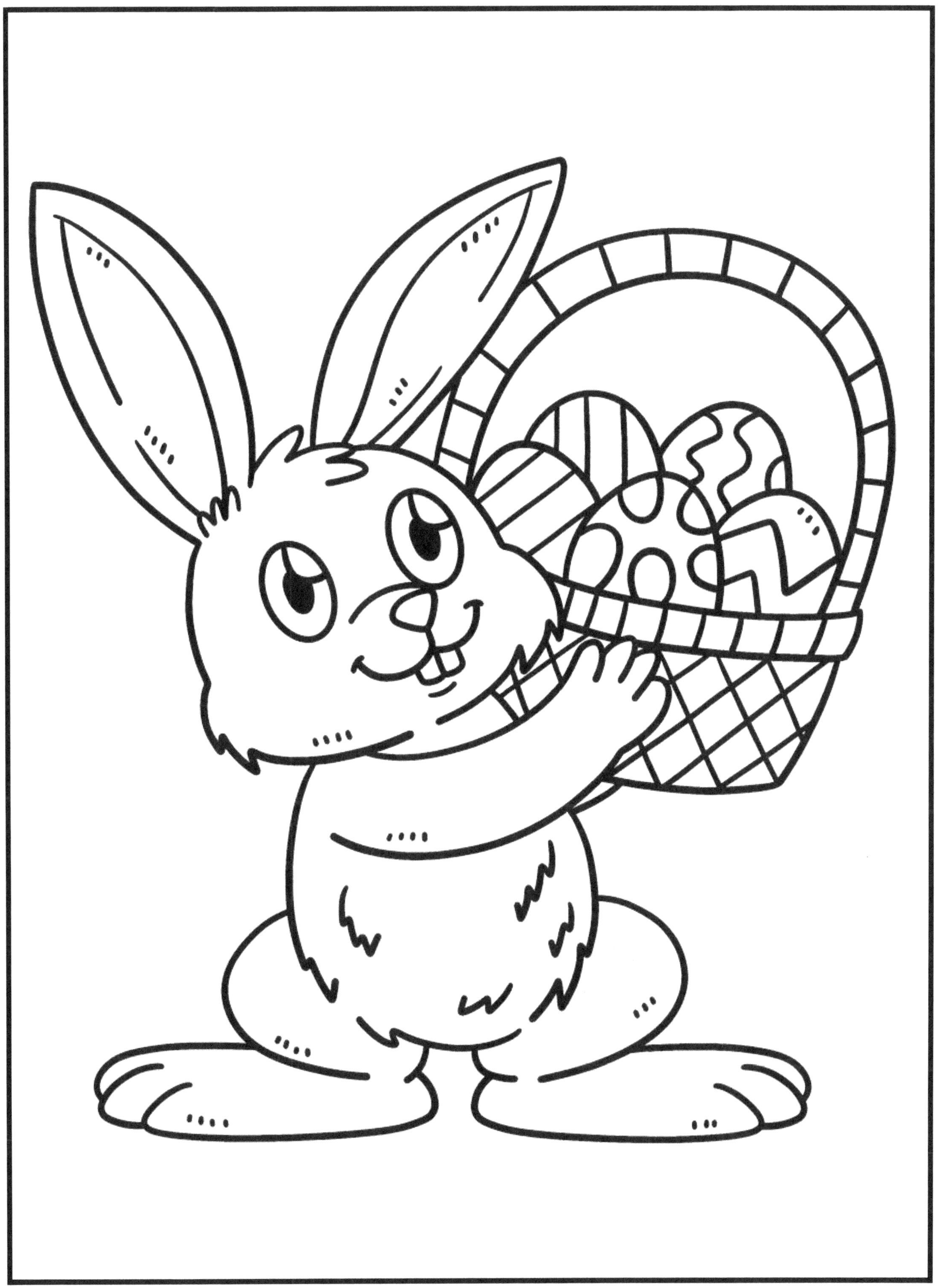

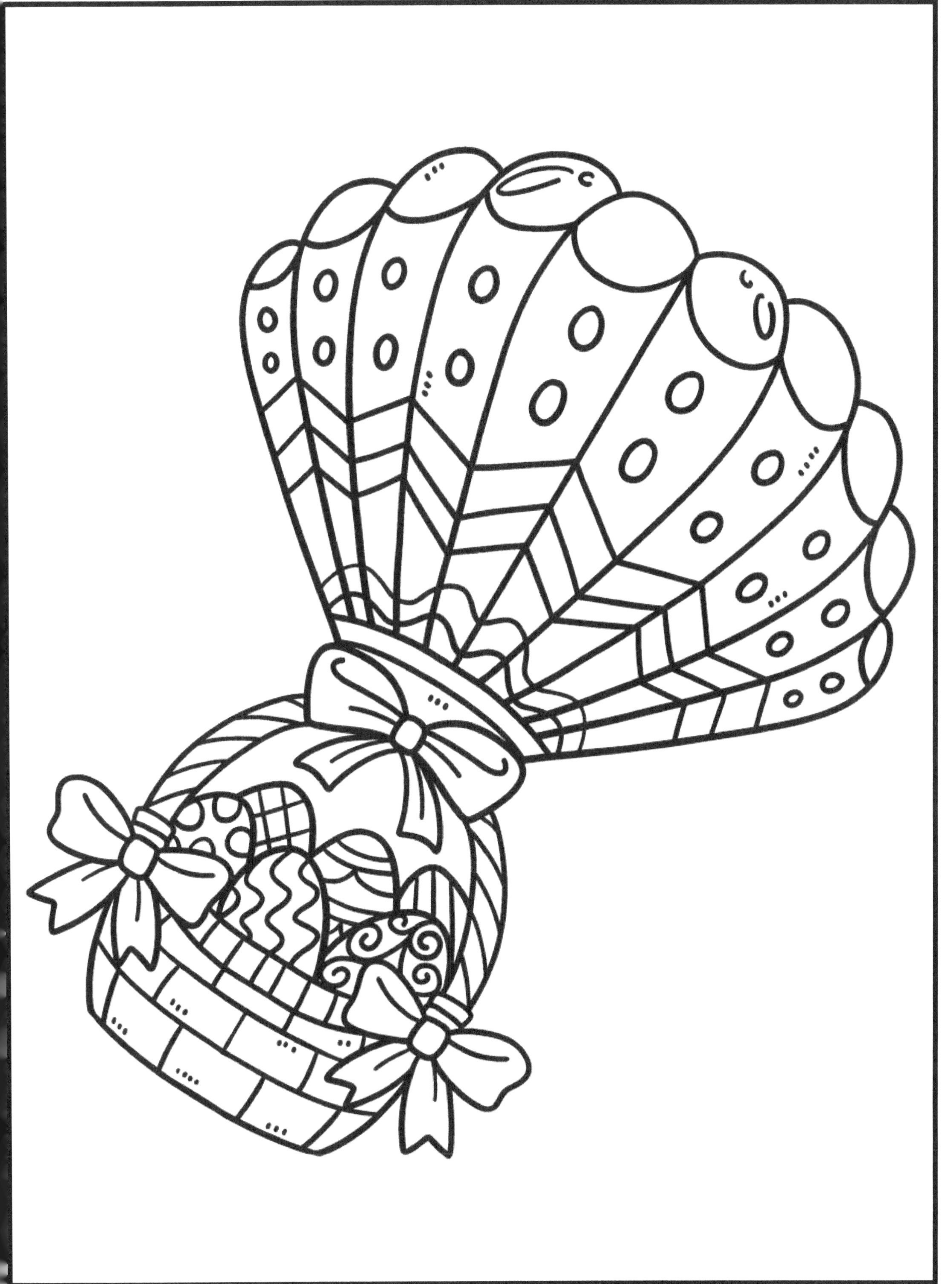

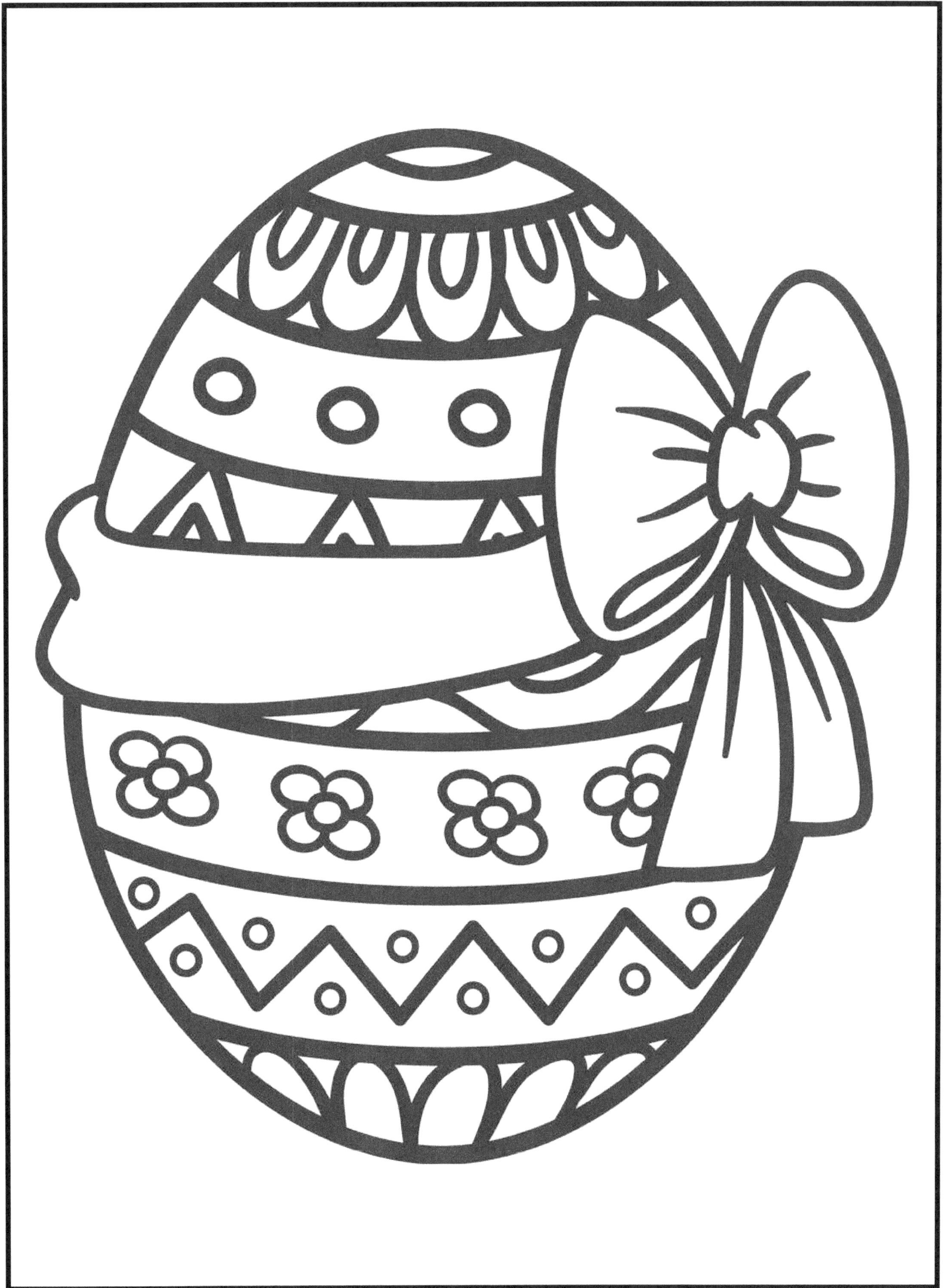

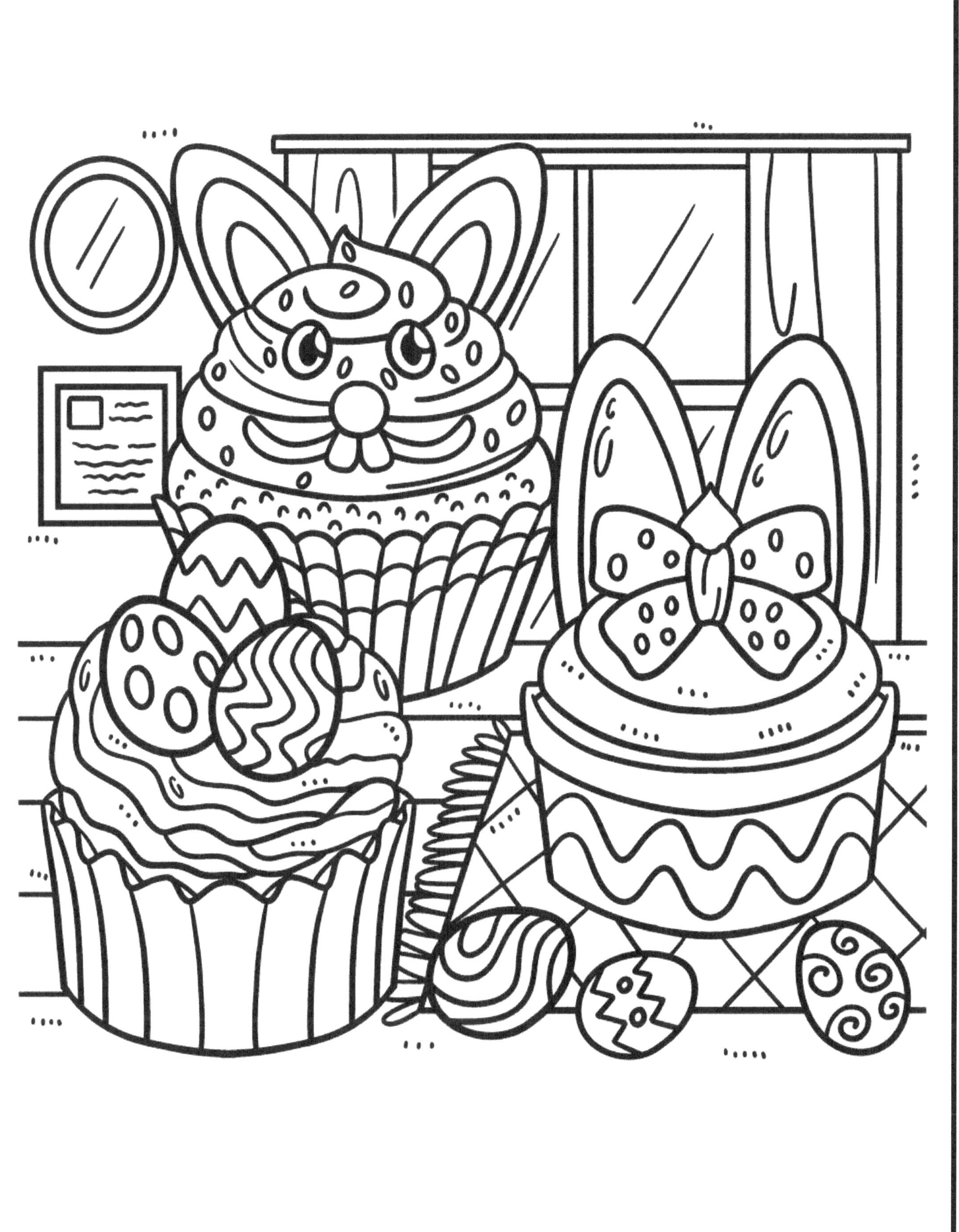

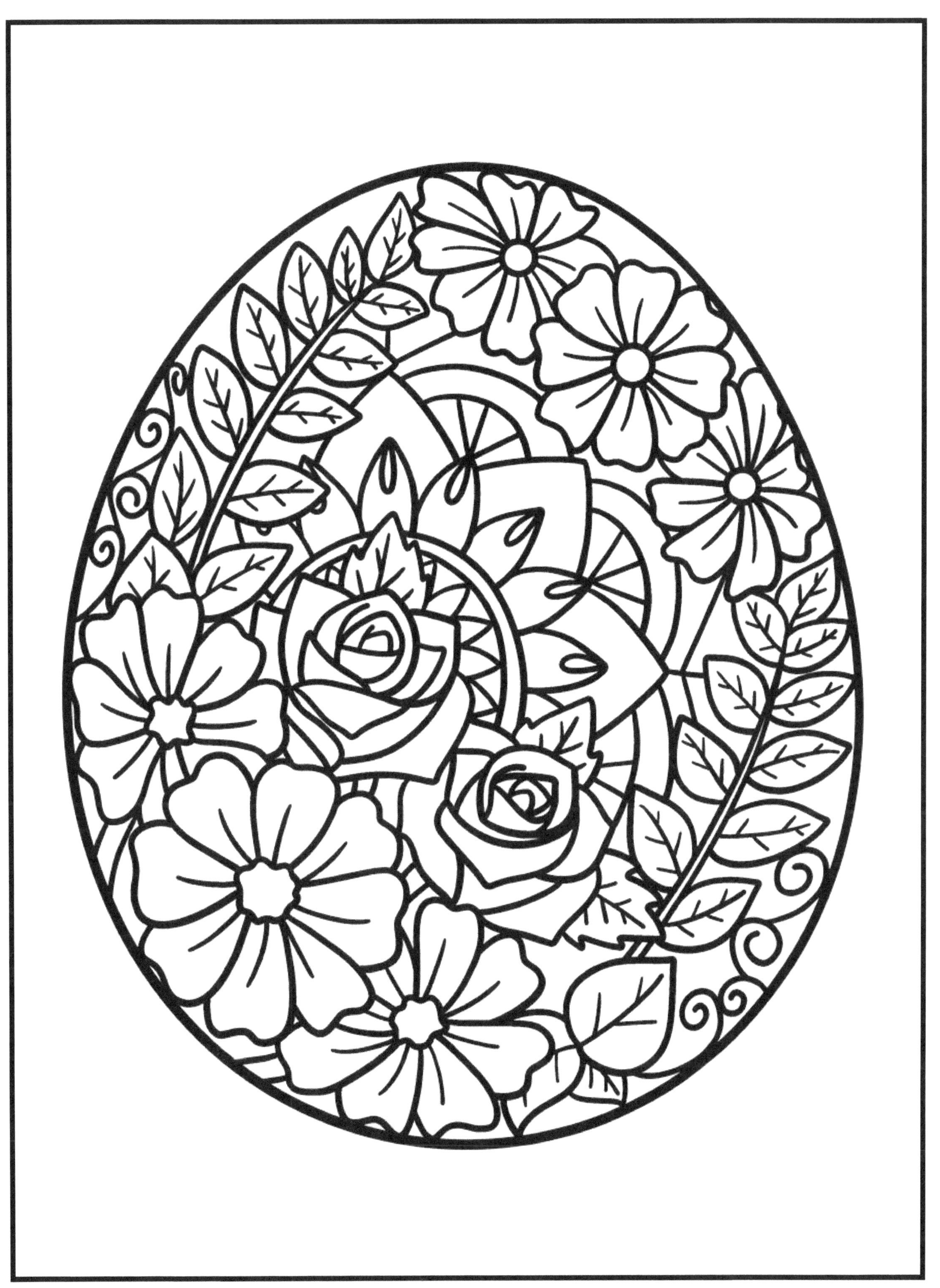

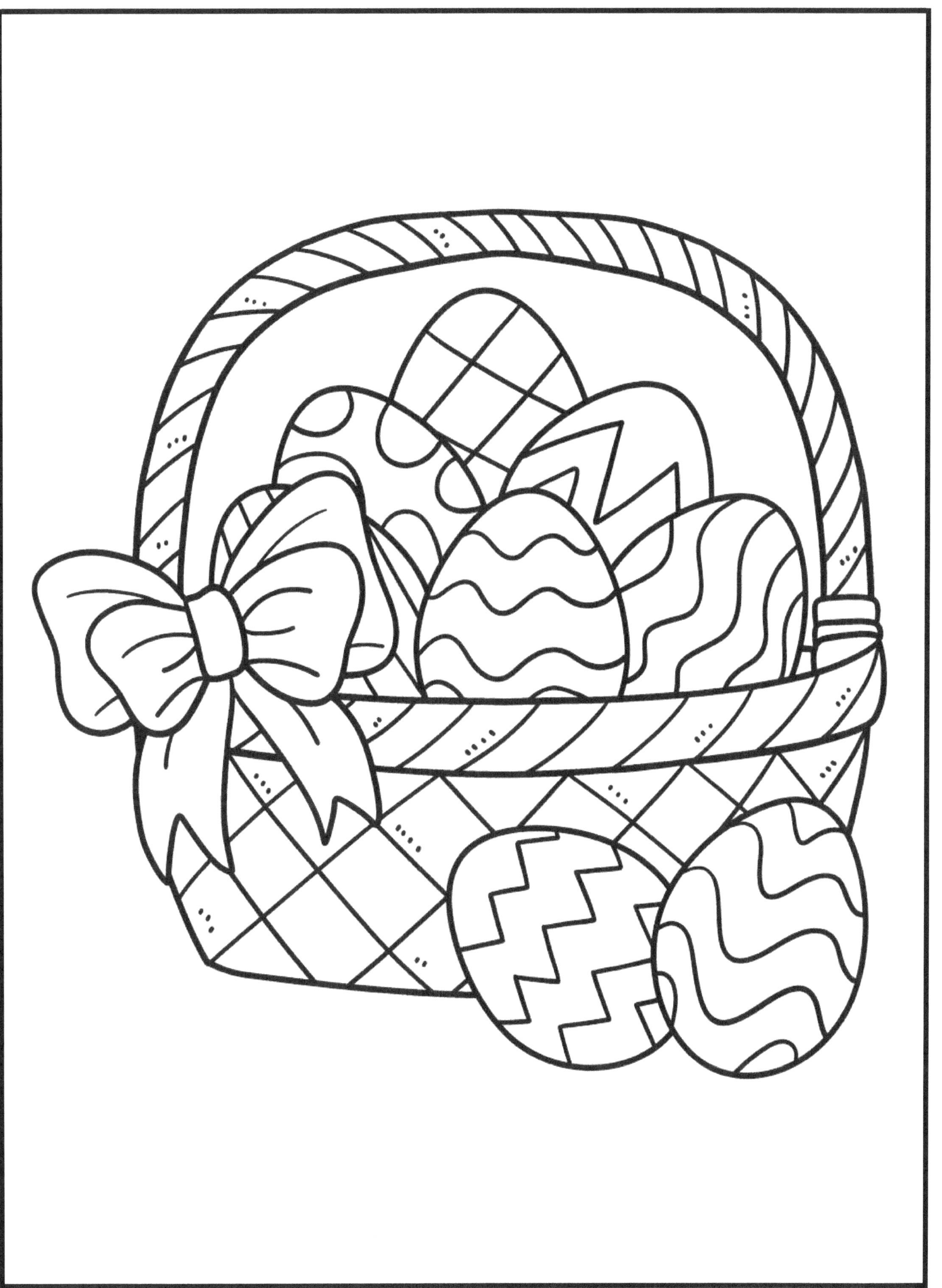

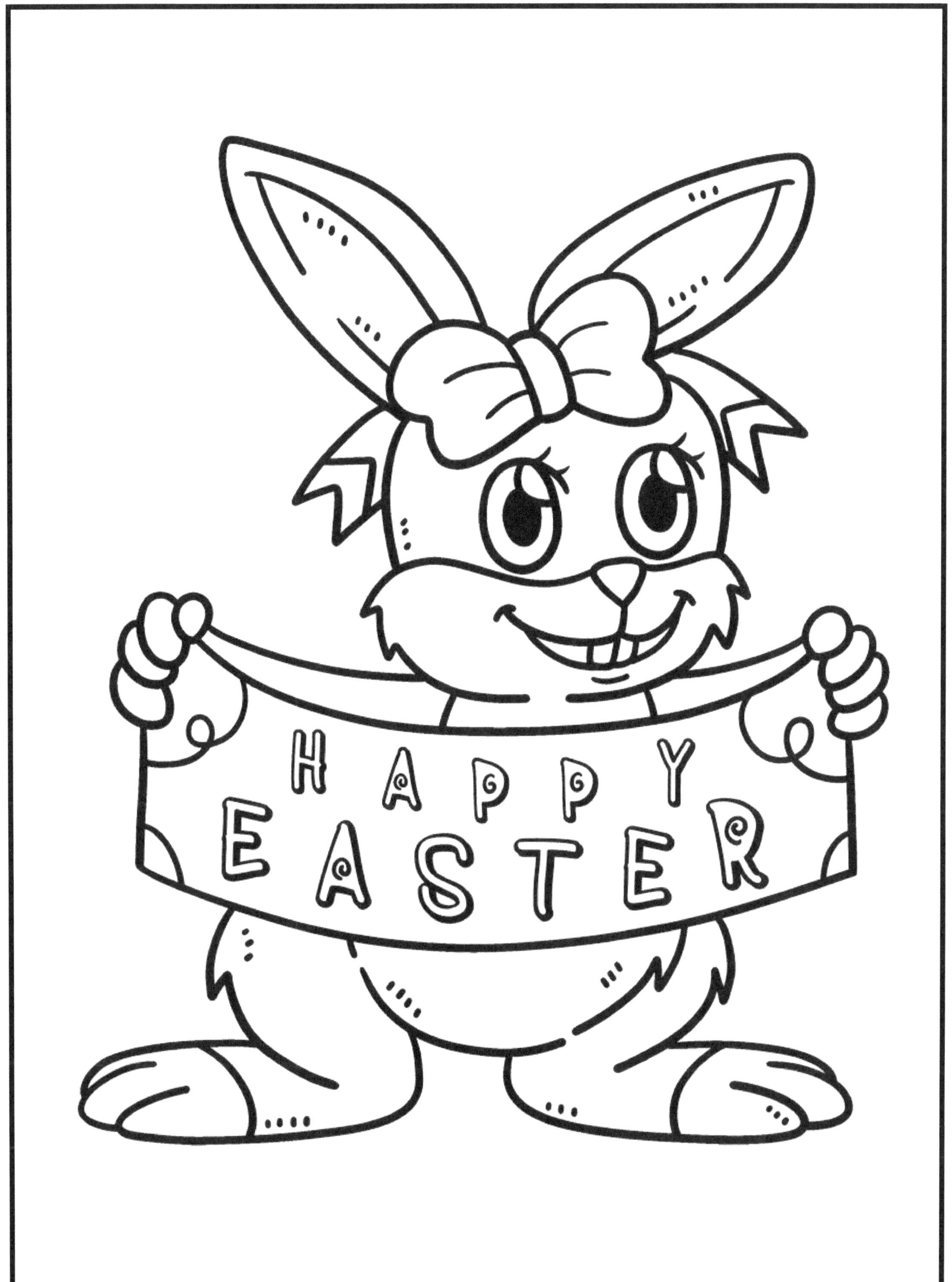

HAPPY
EASTER

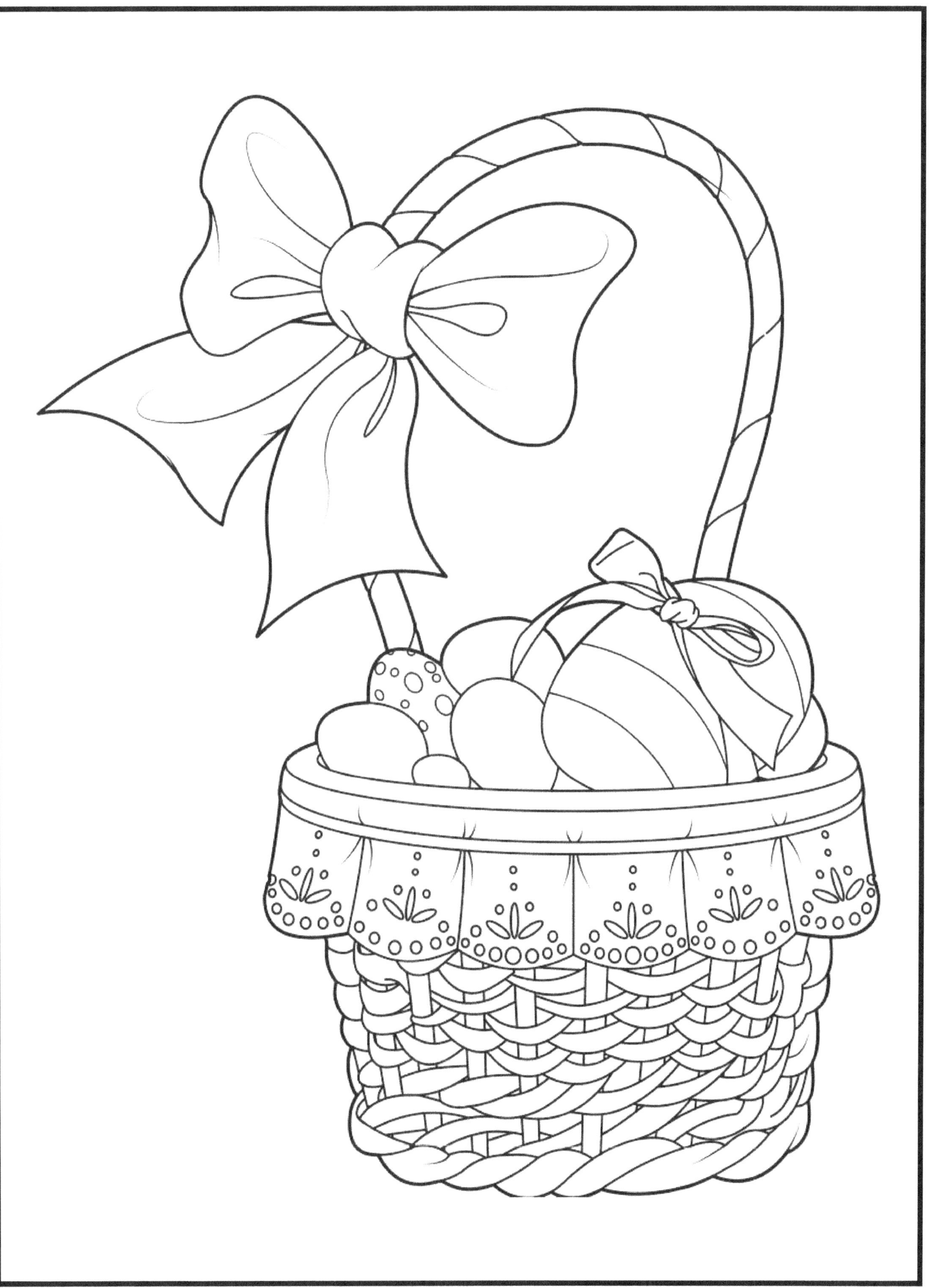

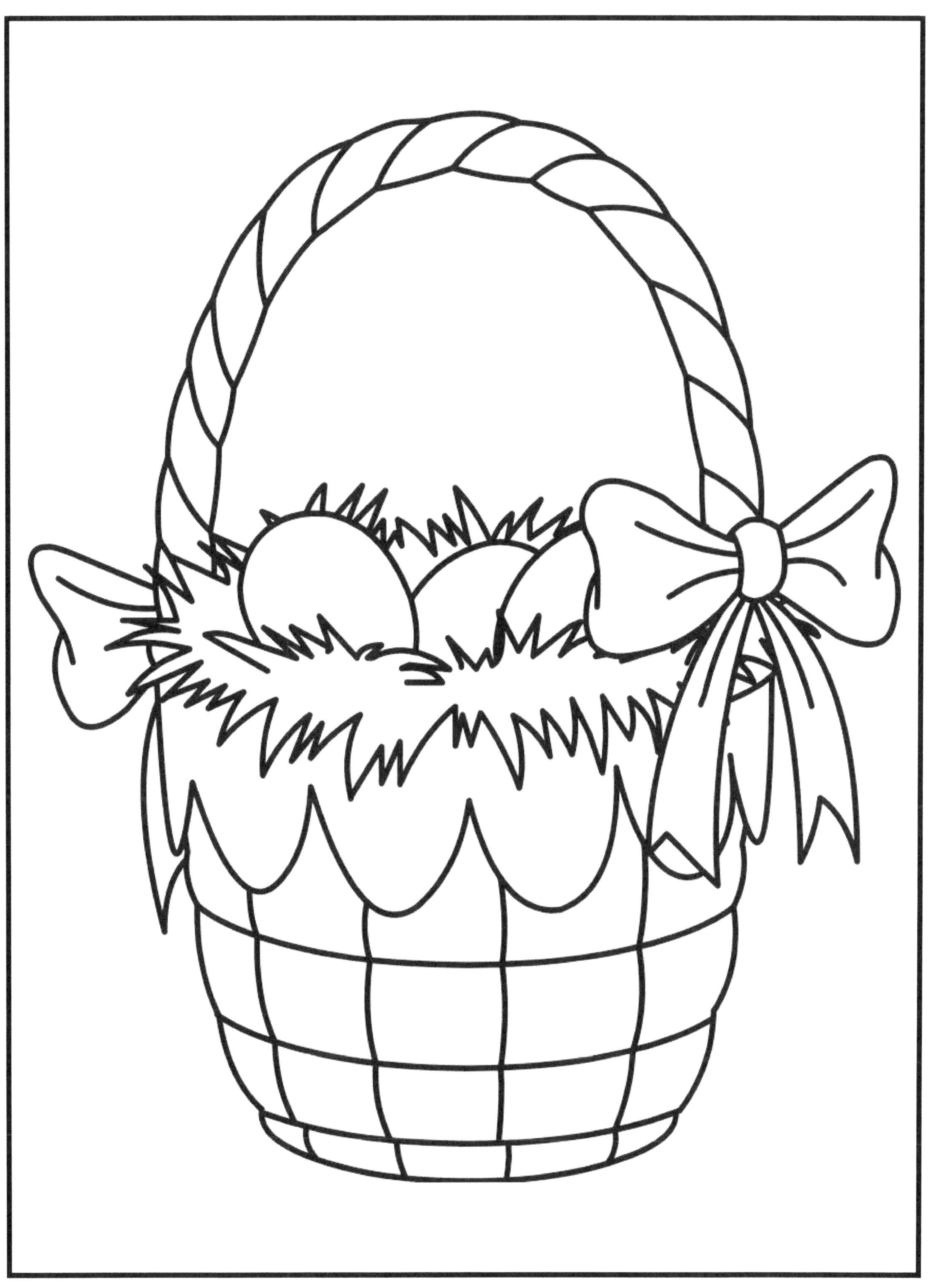

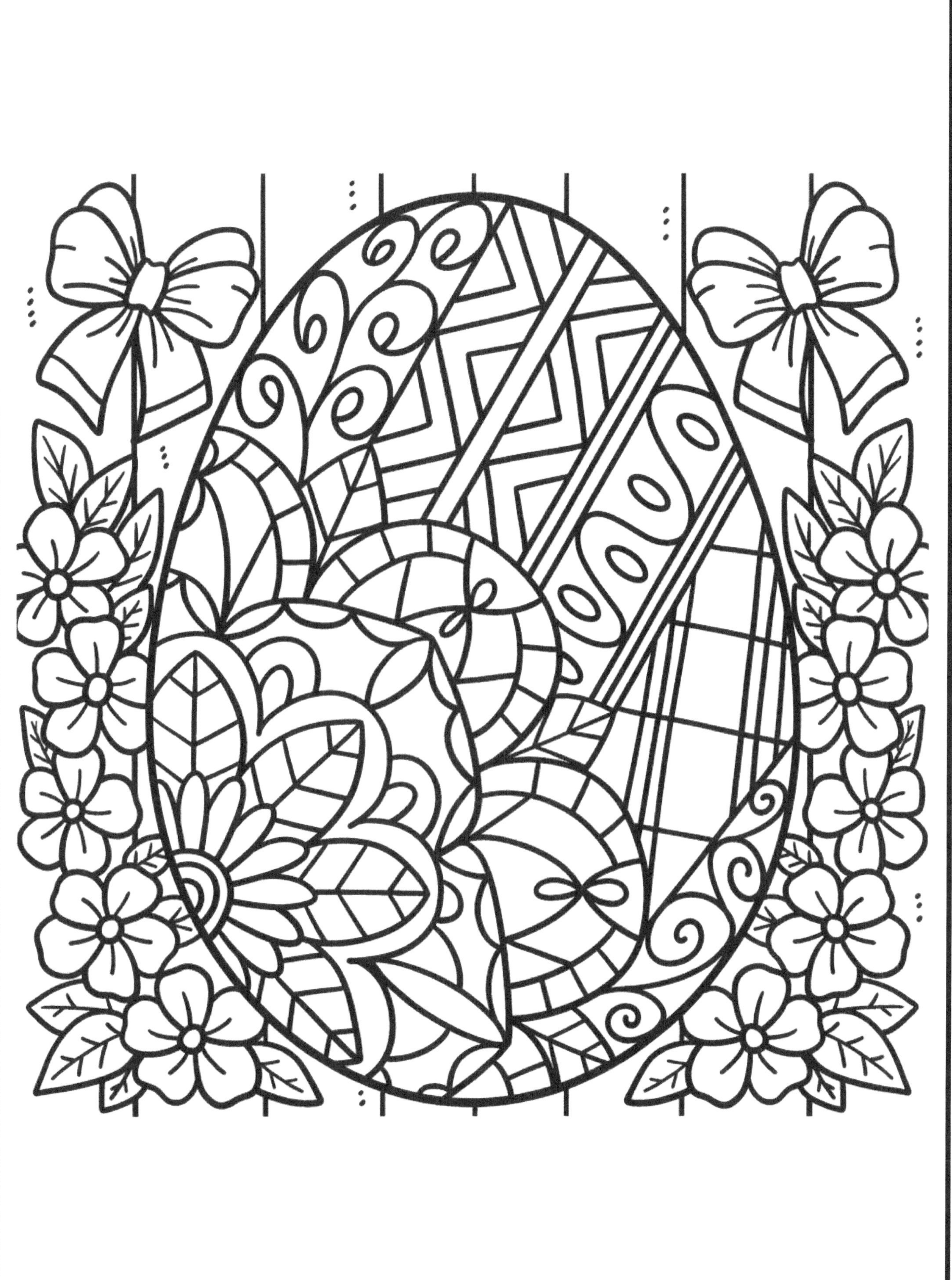

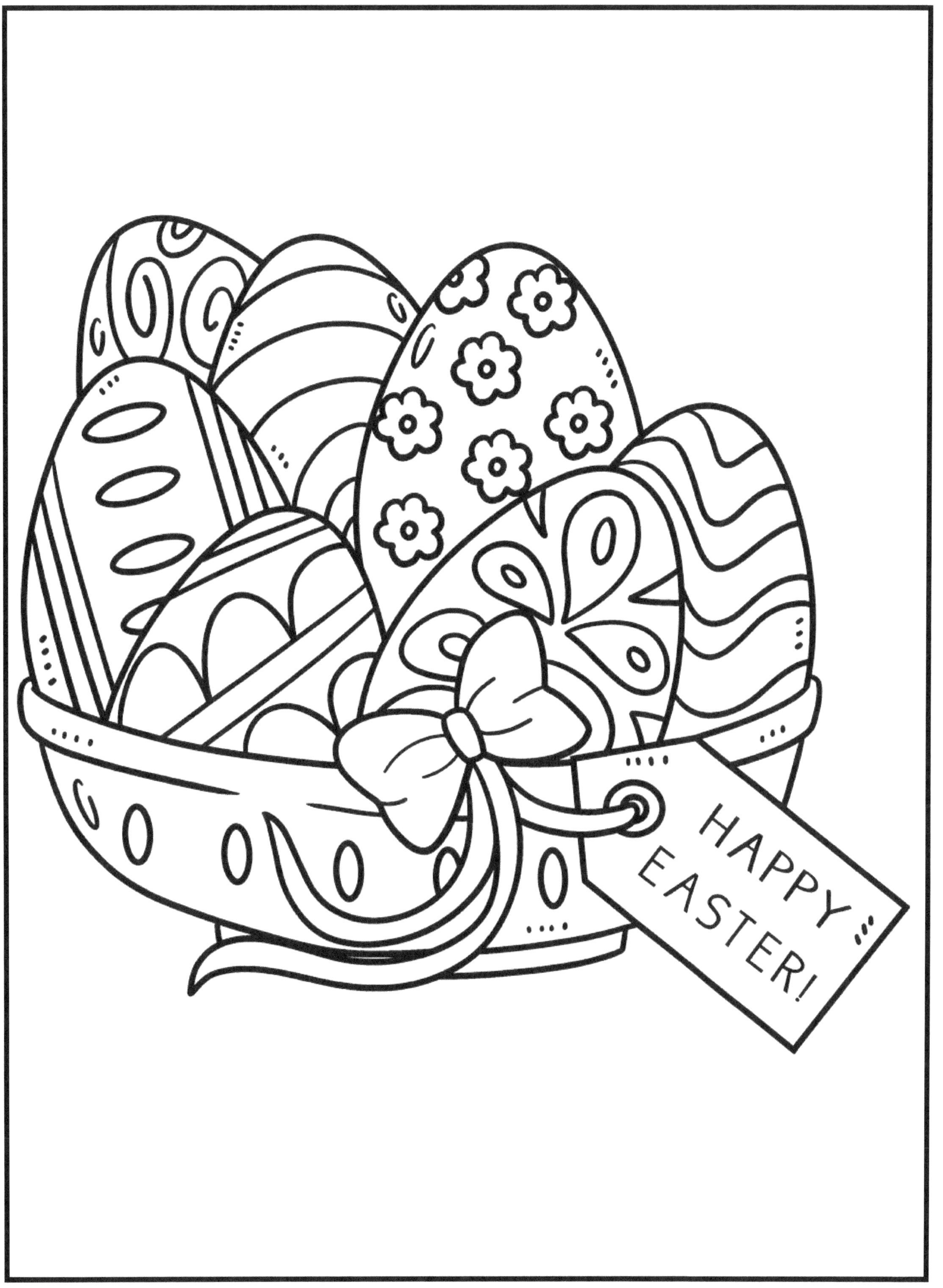
HAPPY EASTER!

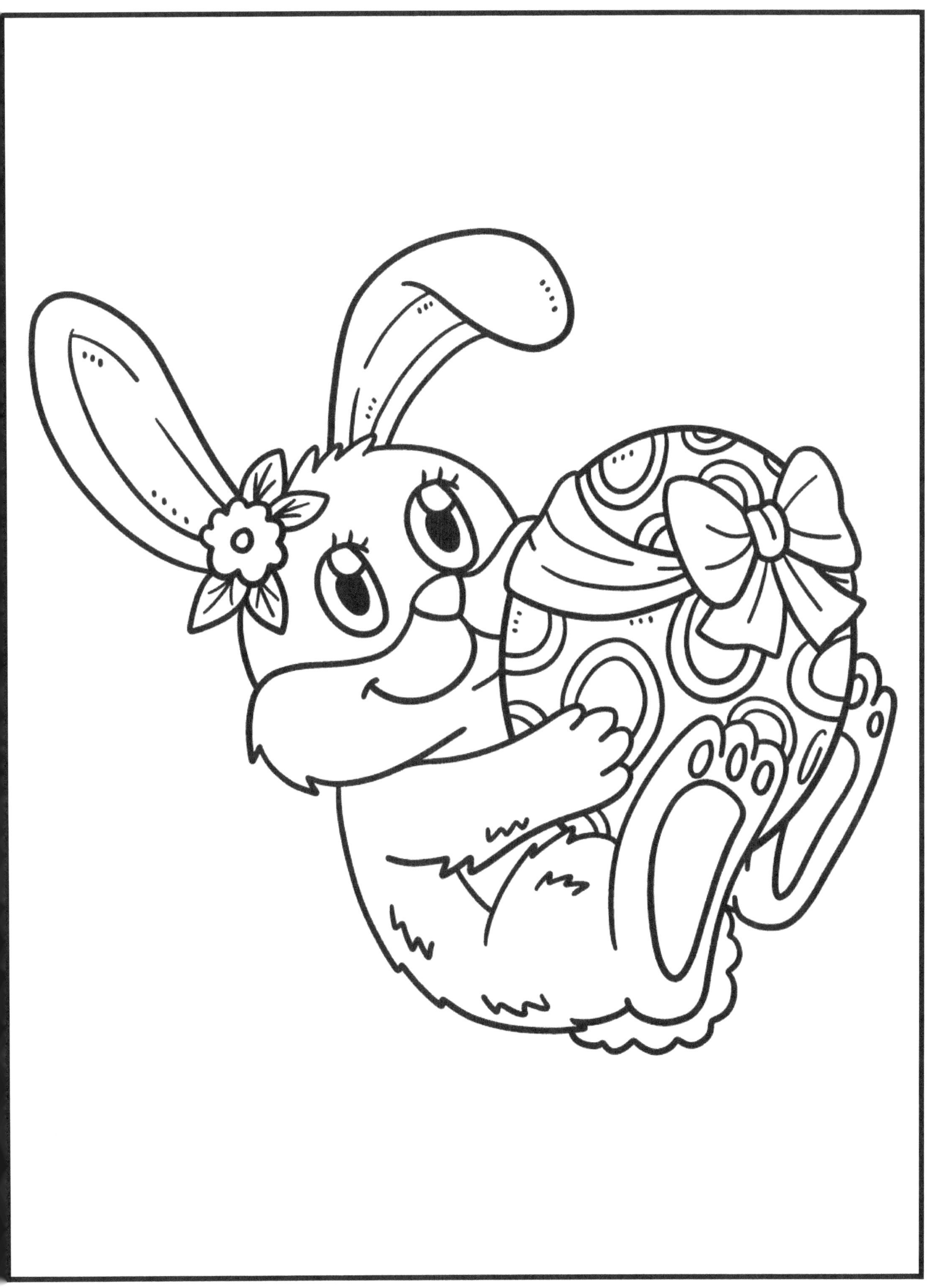

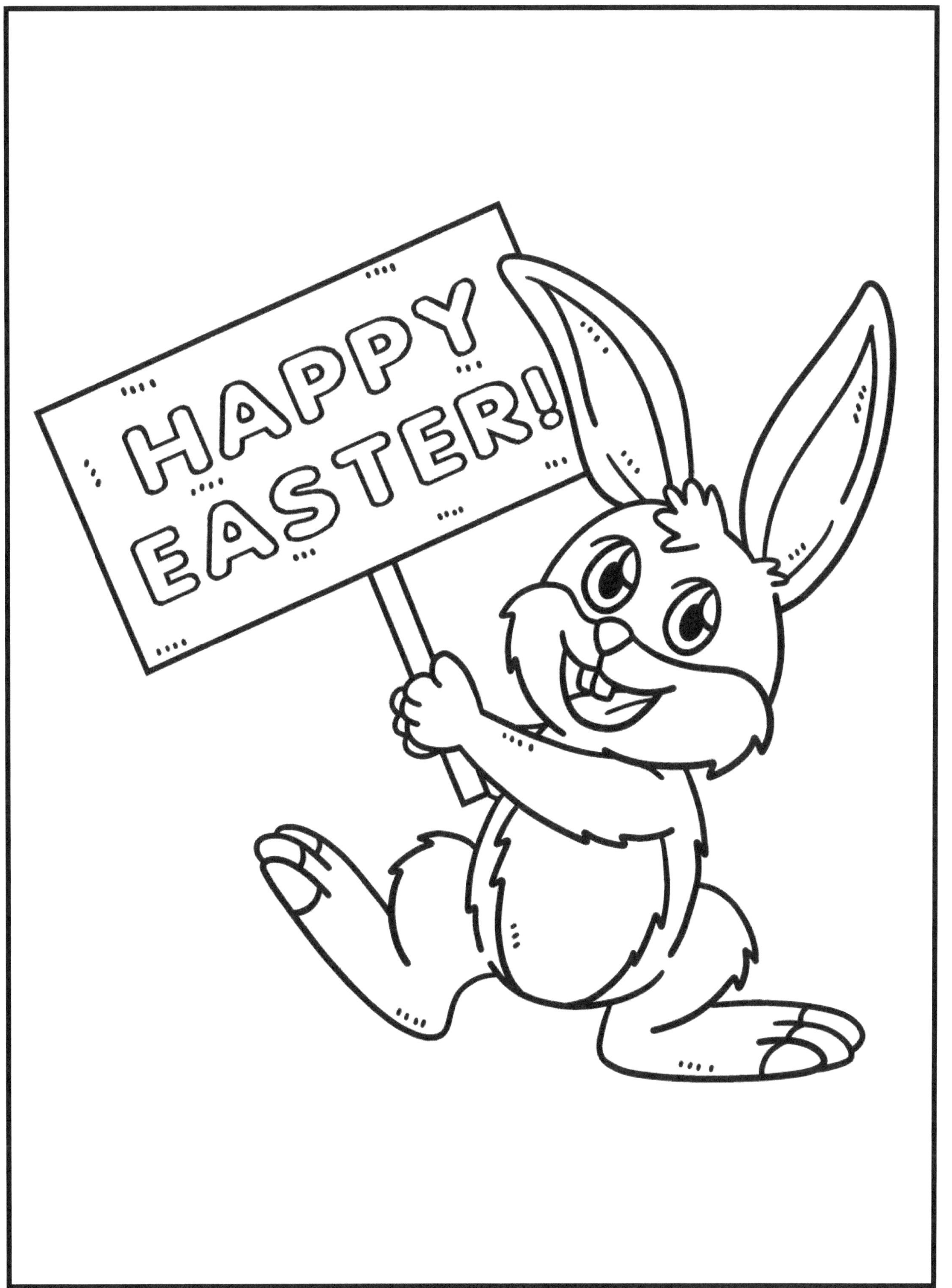

HAPPY
EASTER!

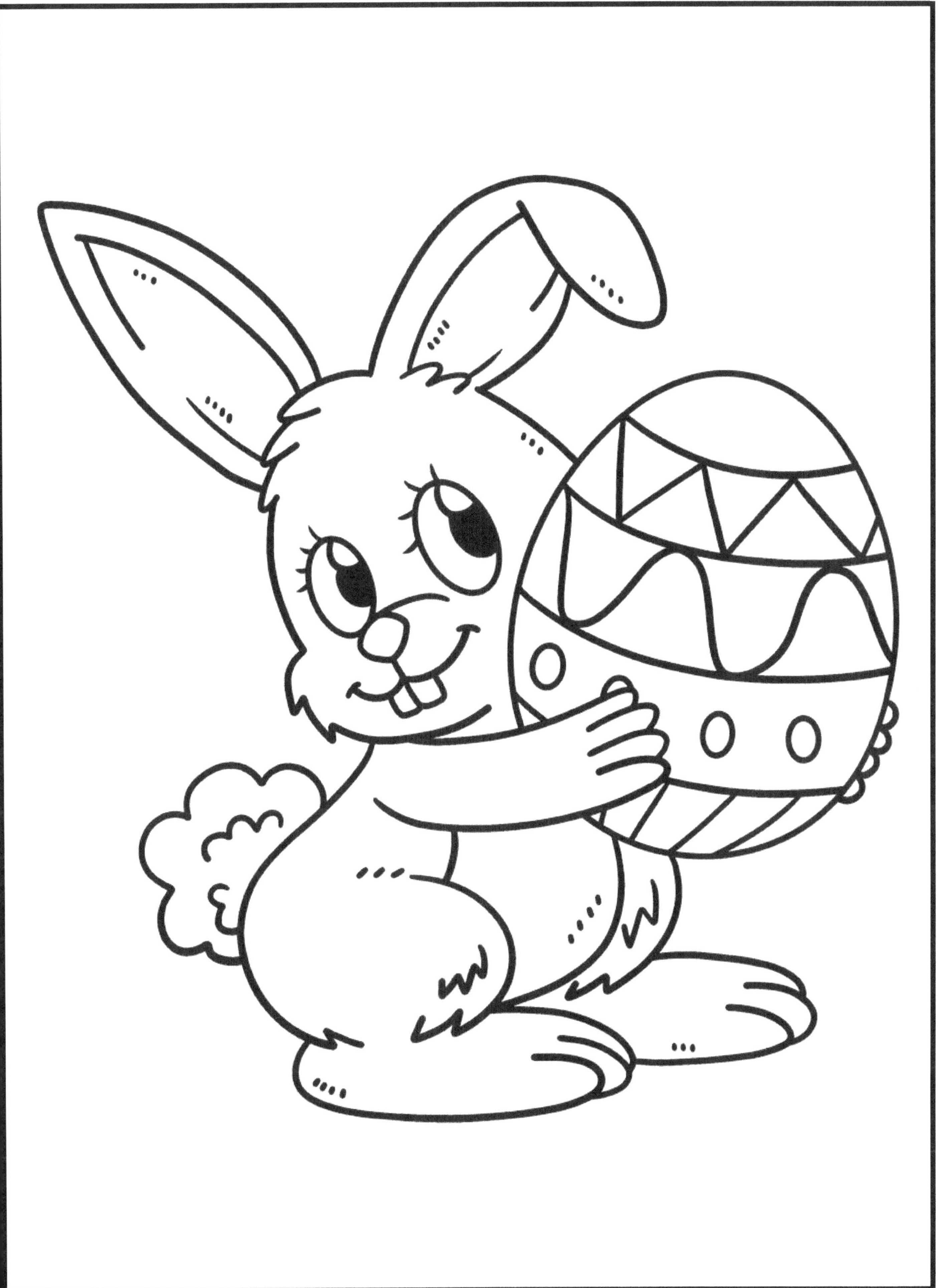

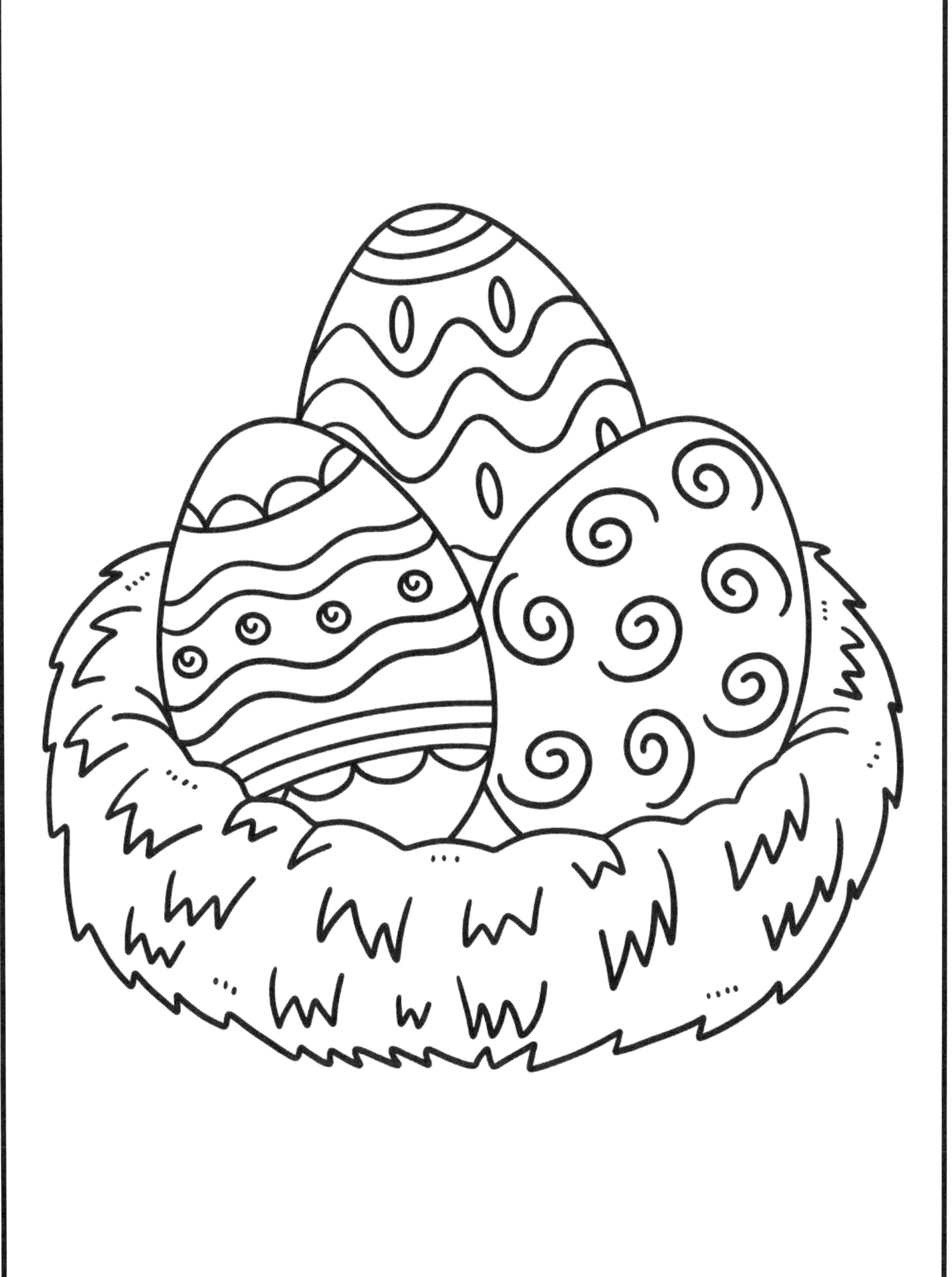

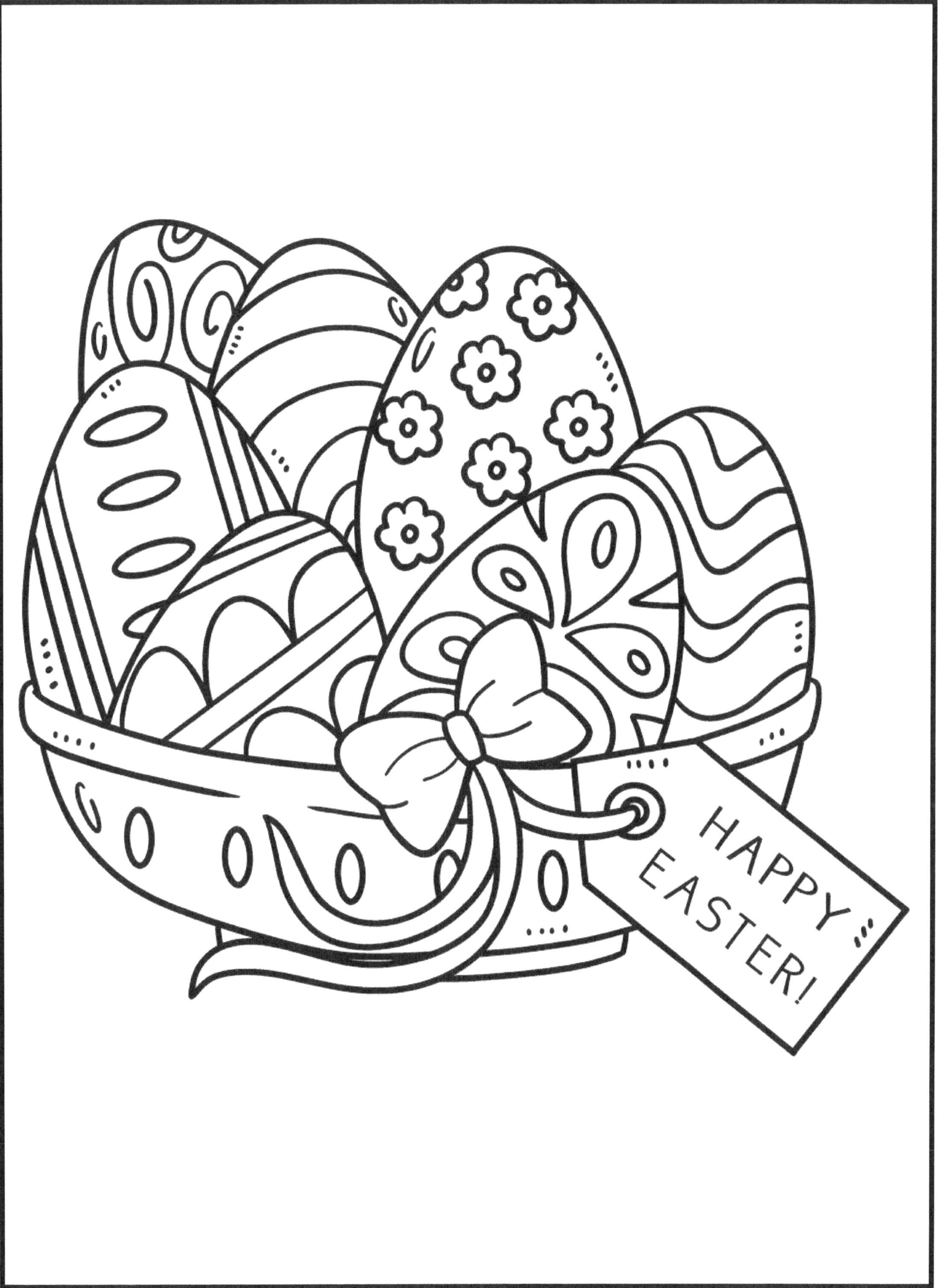
HAPPY EASTER!

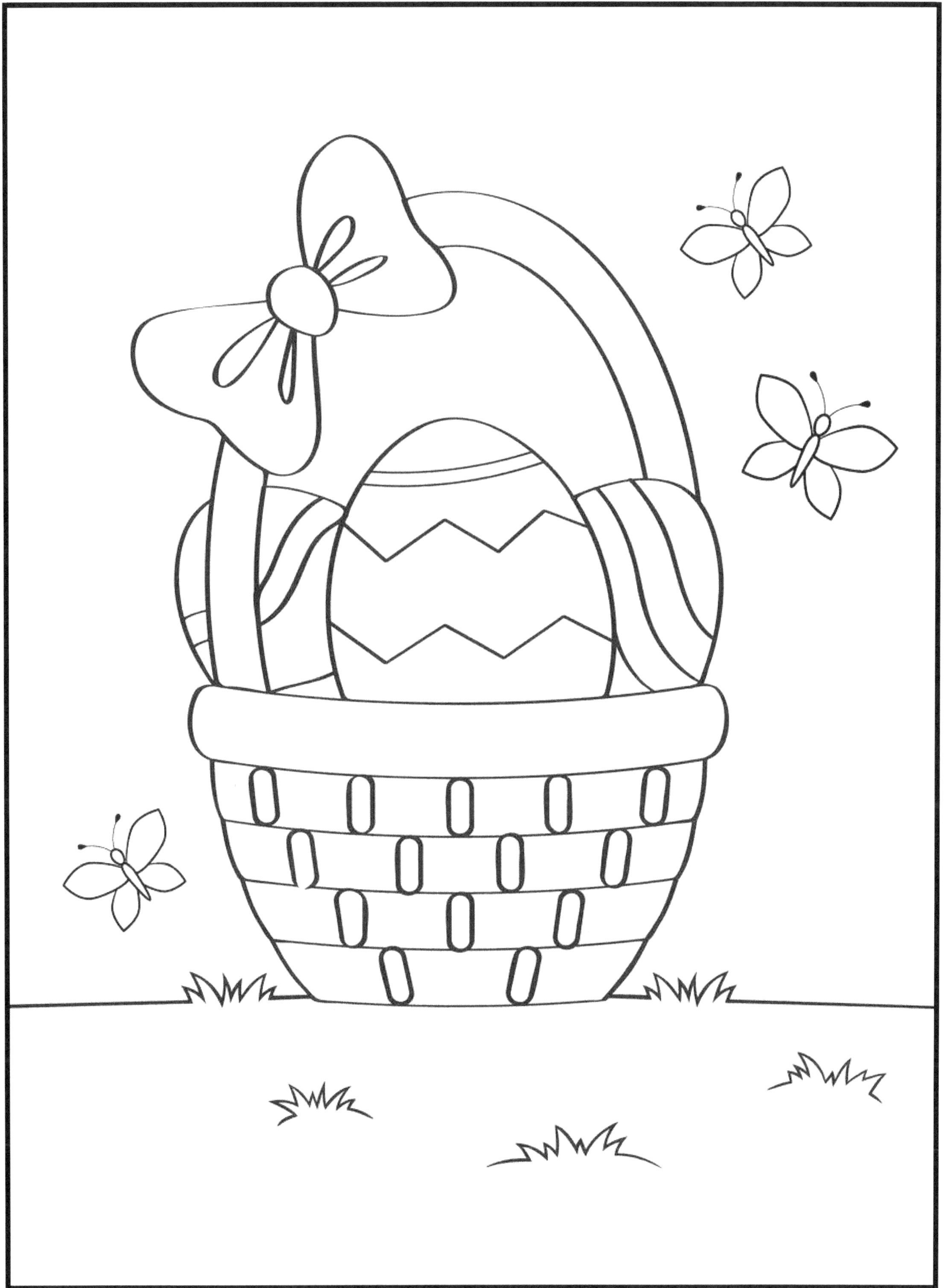

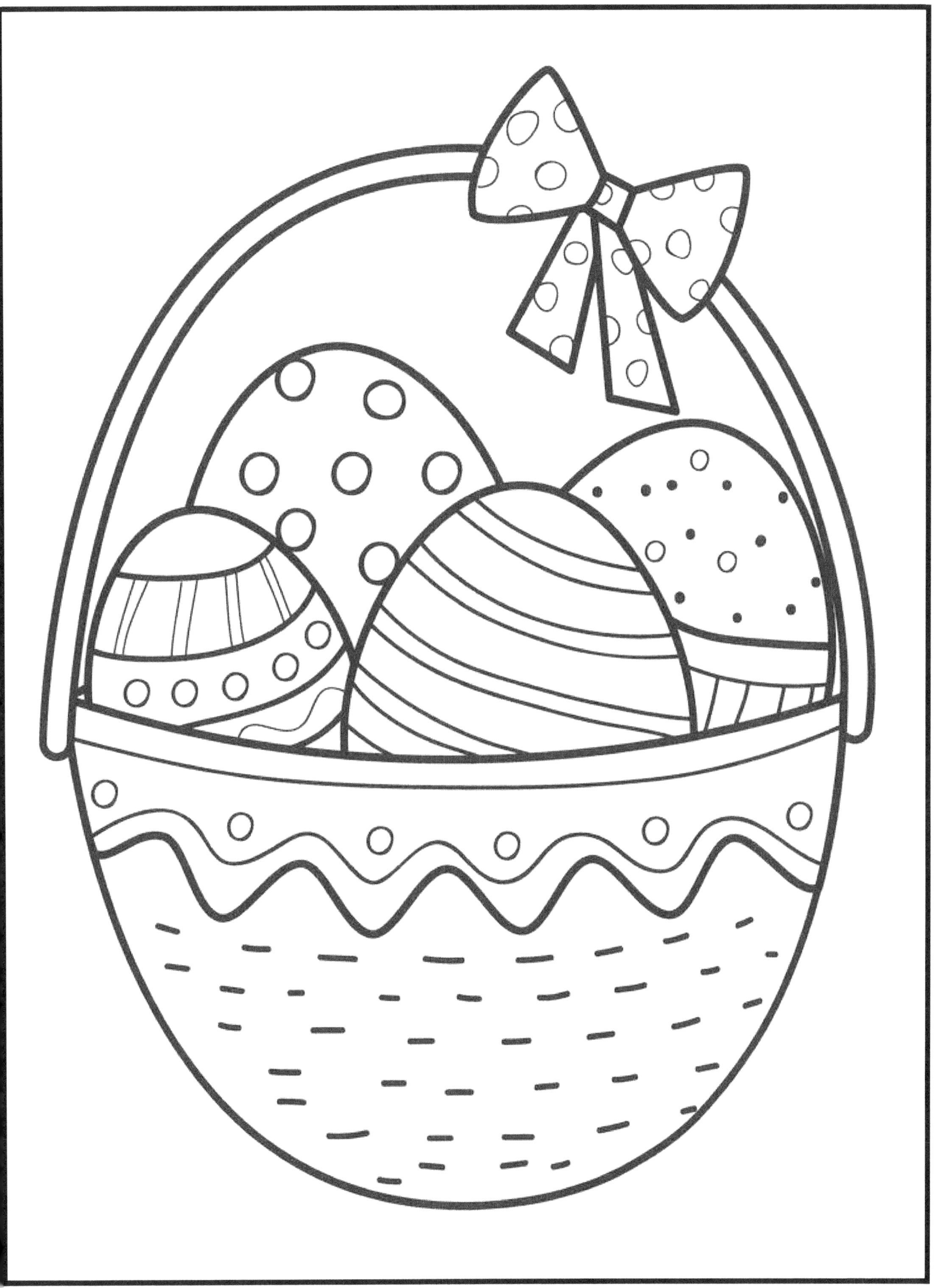

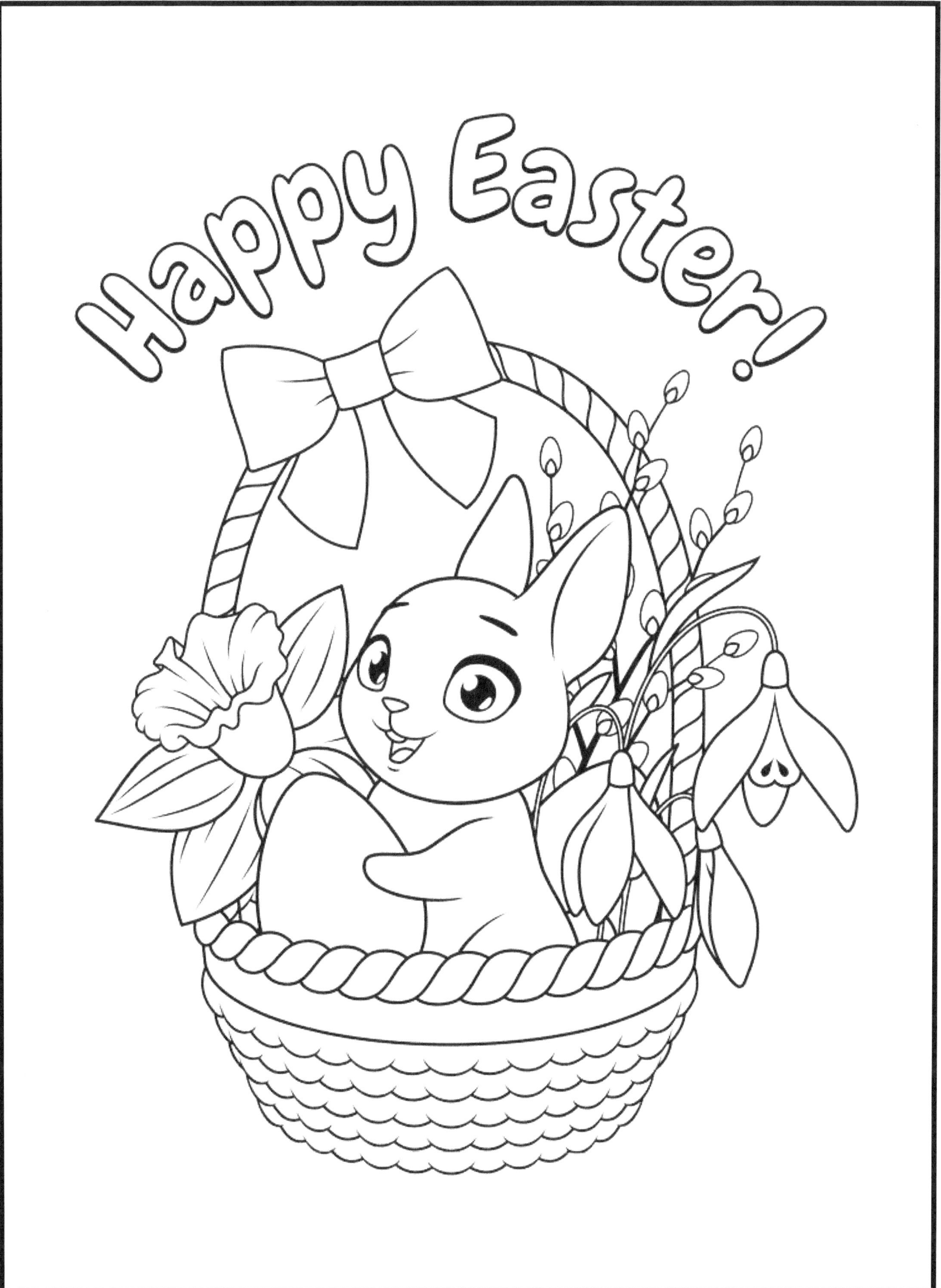
Happy Easter!

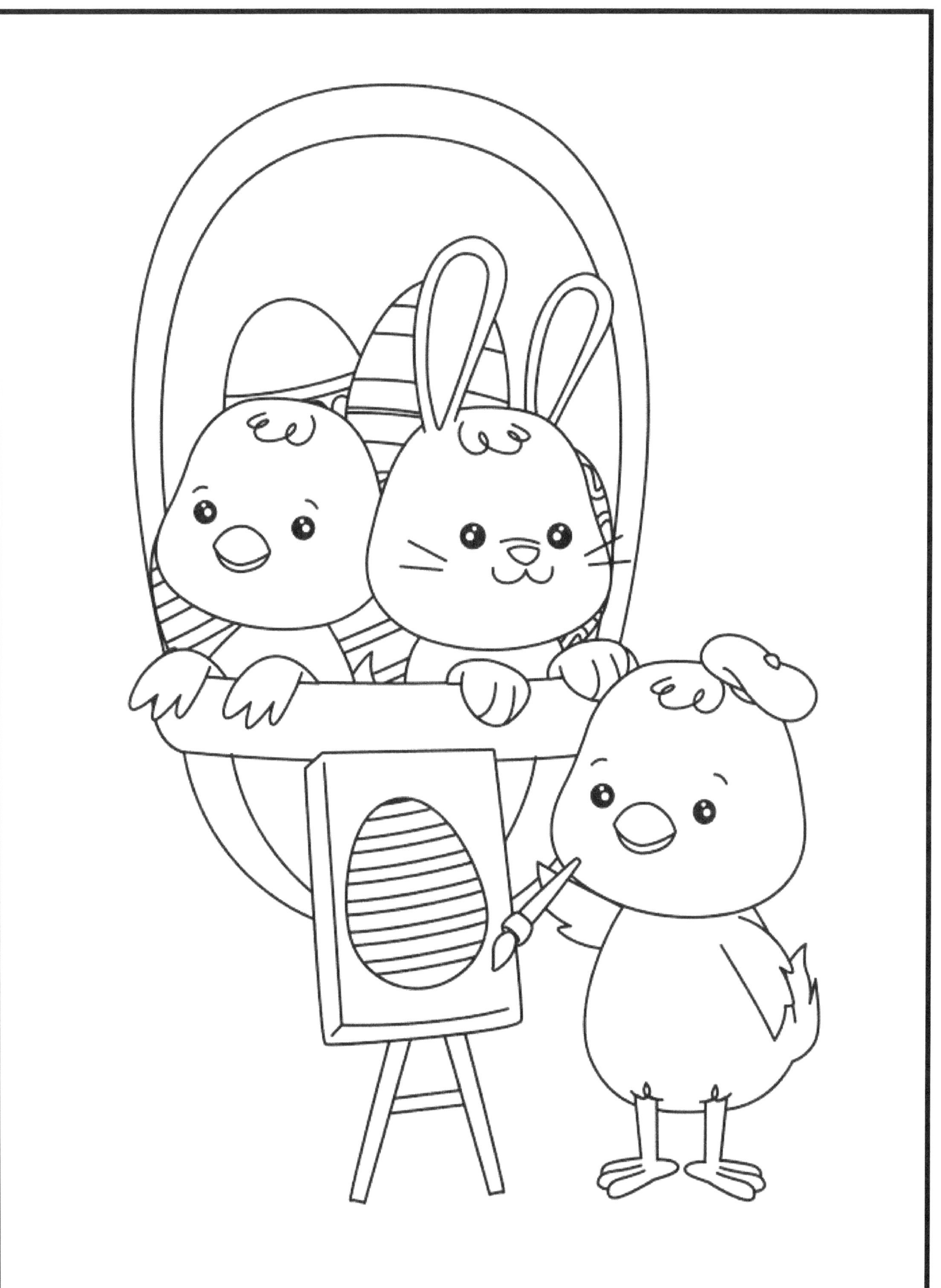

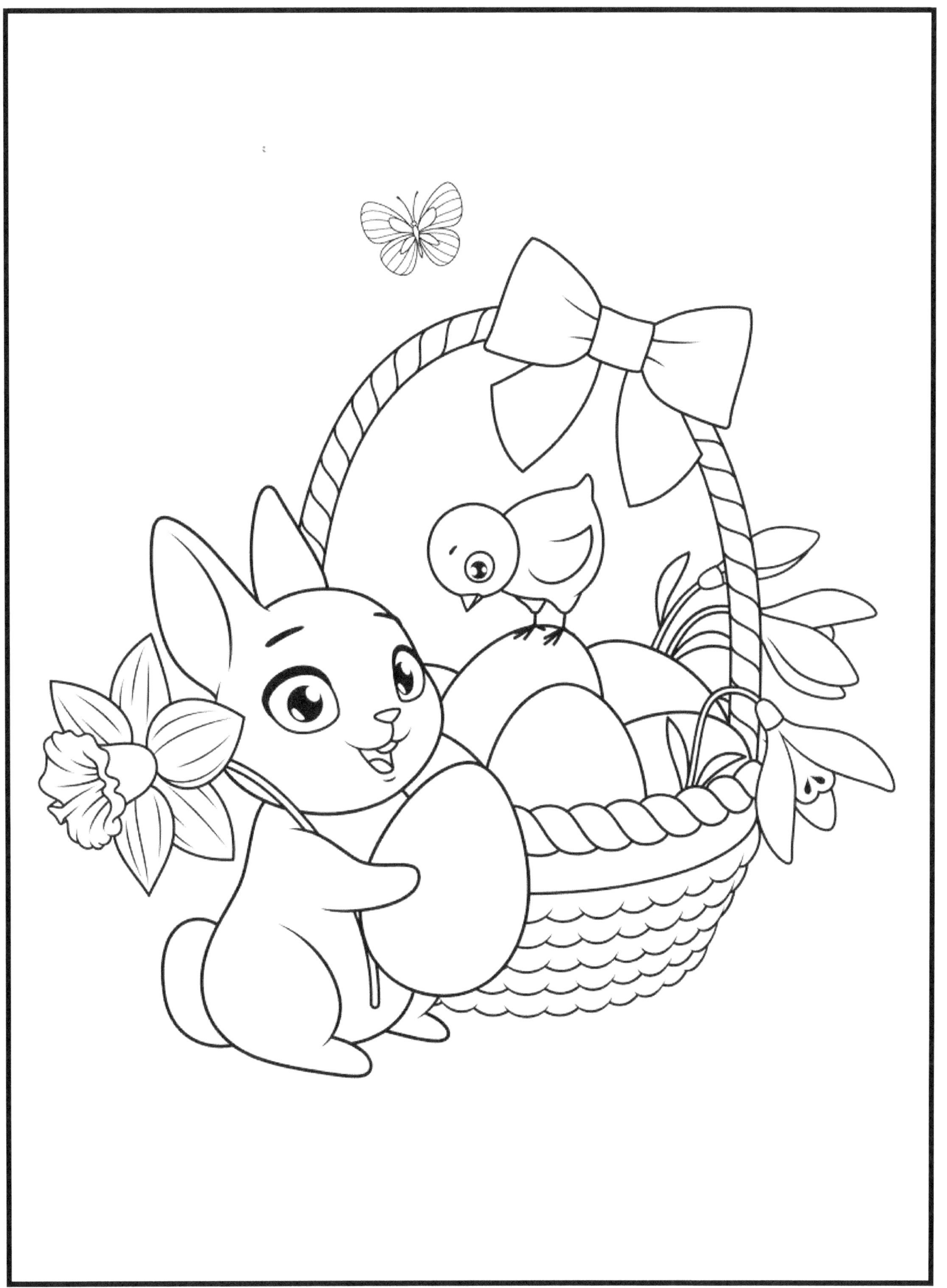

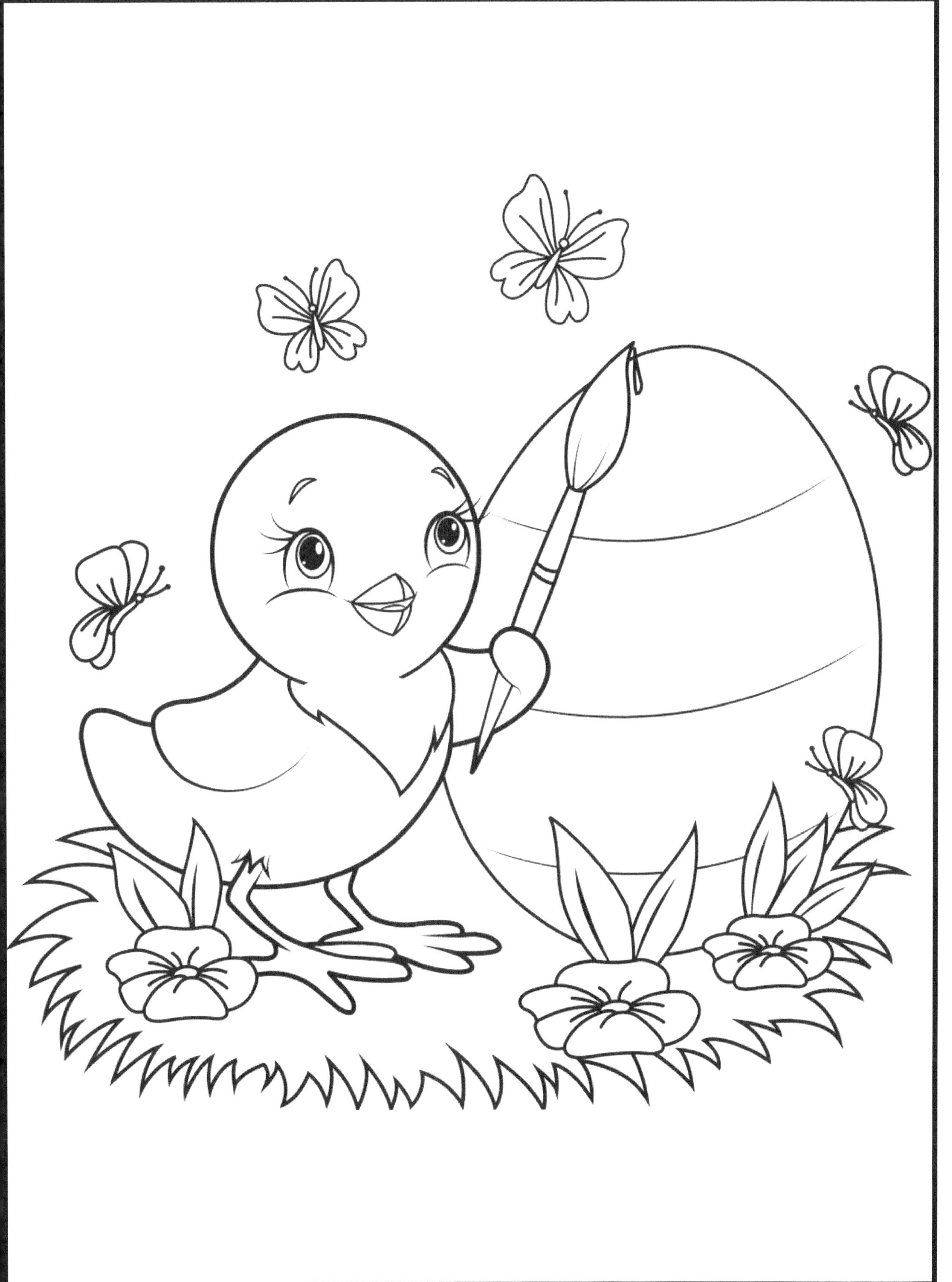

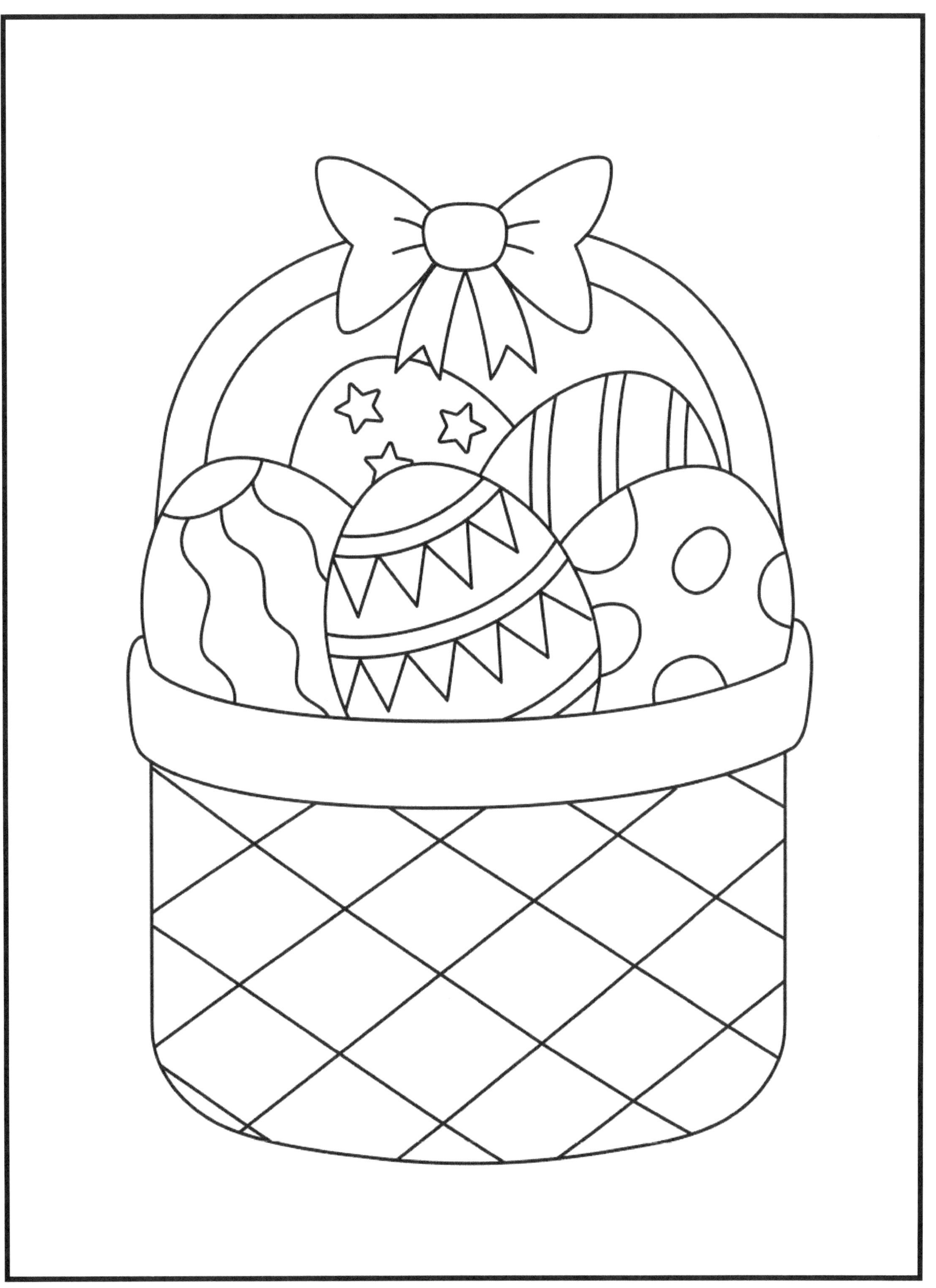

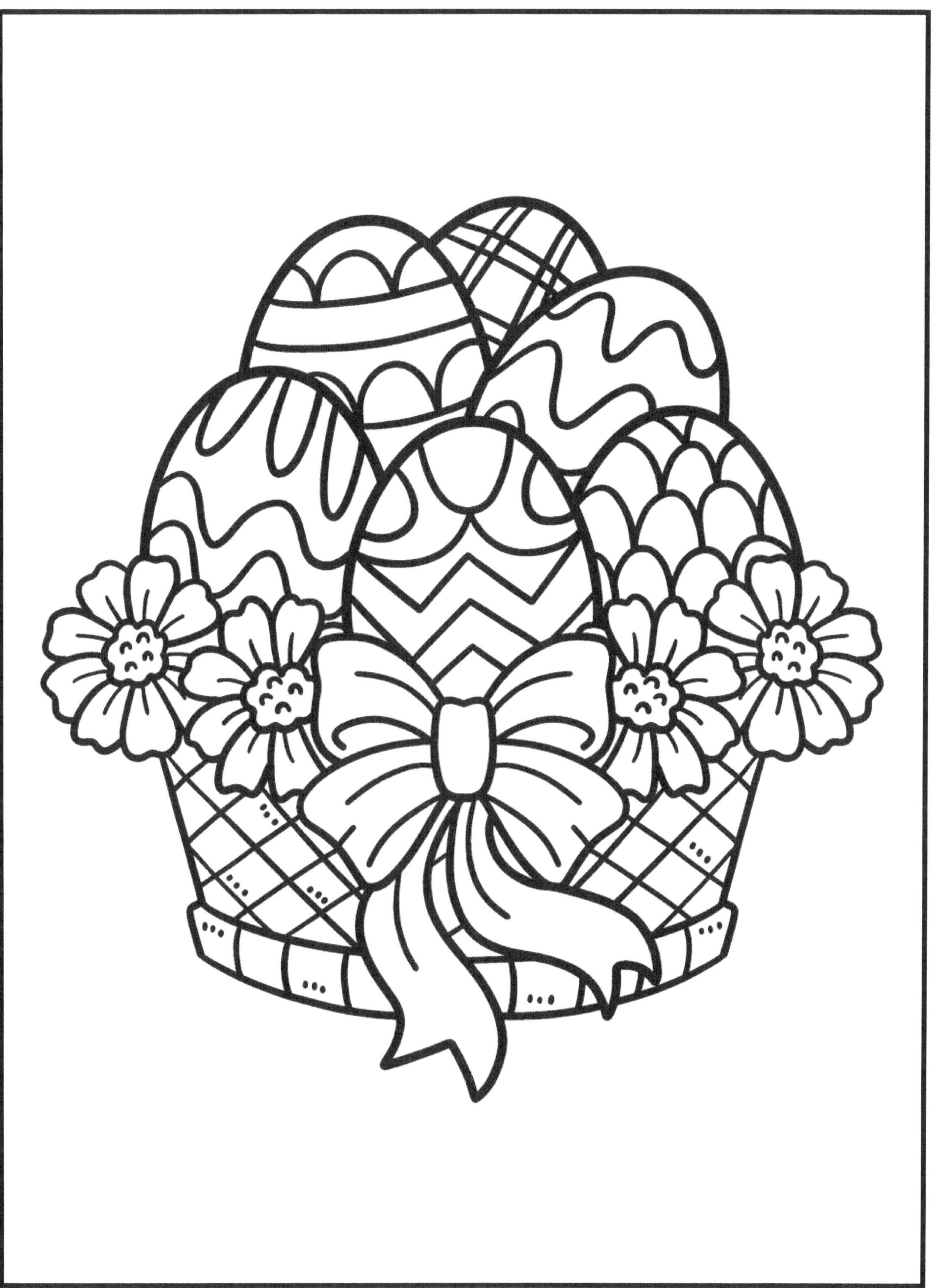

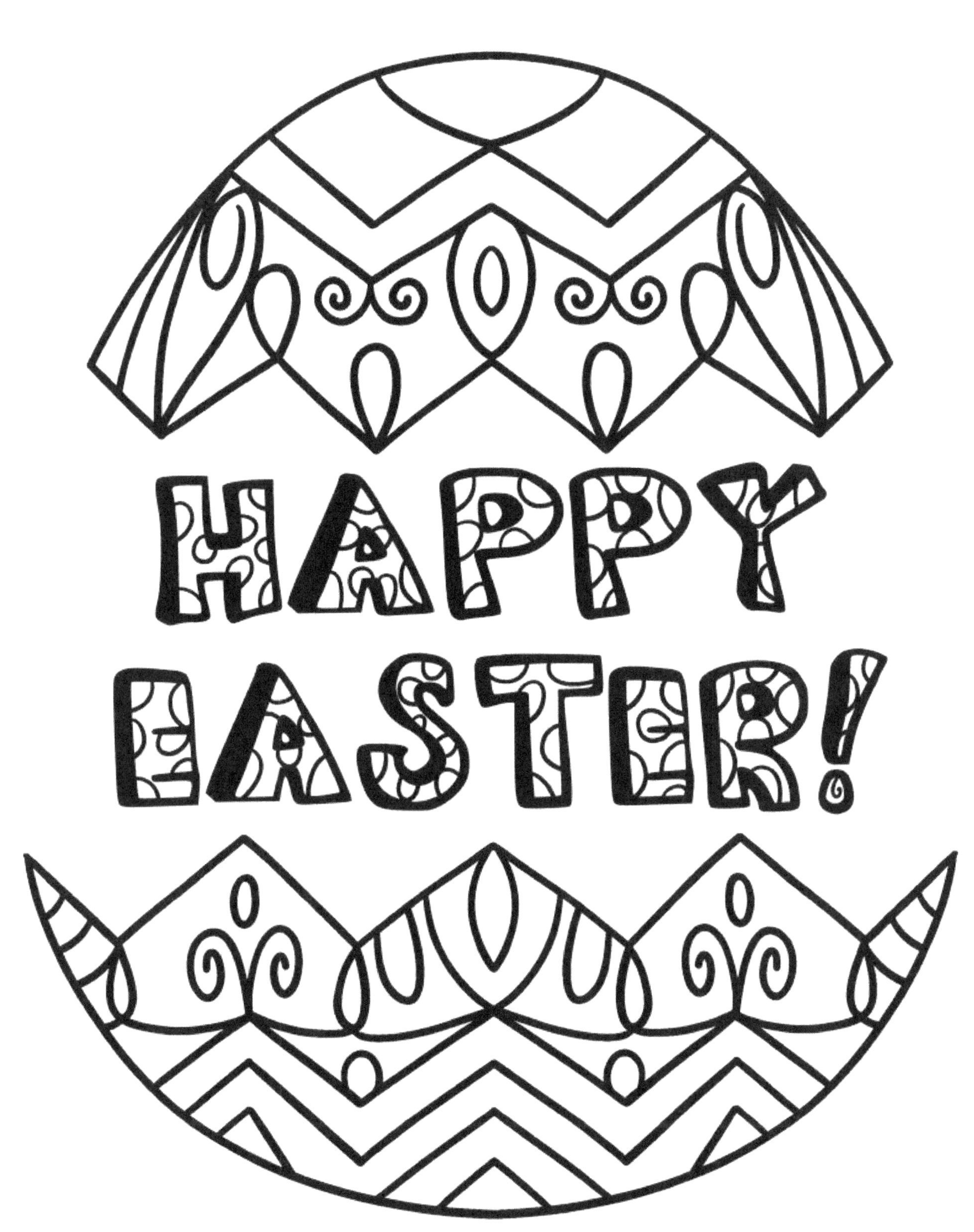

HAPPY EASTER!

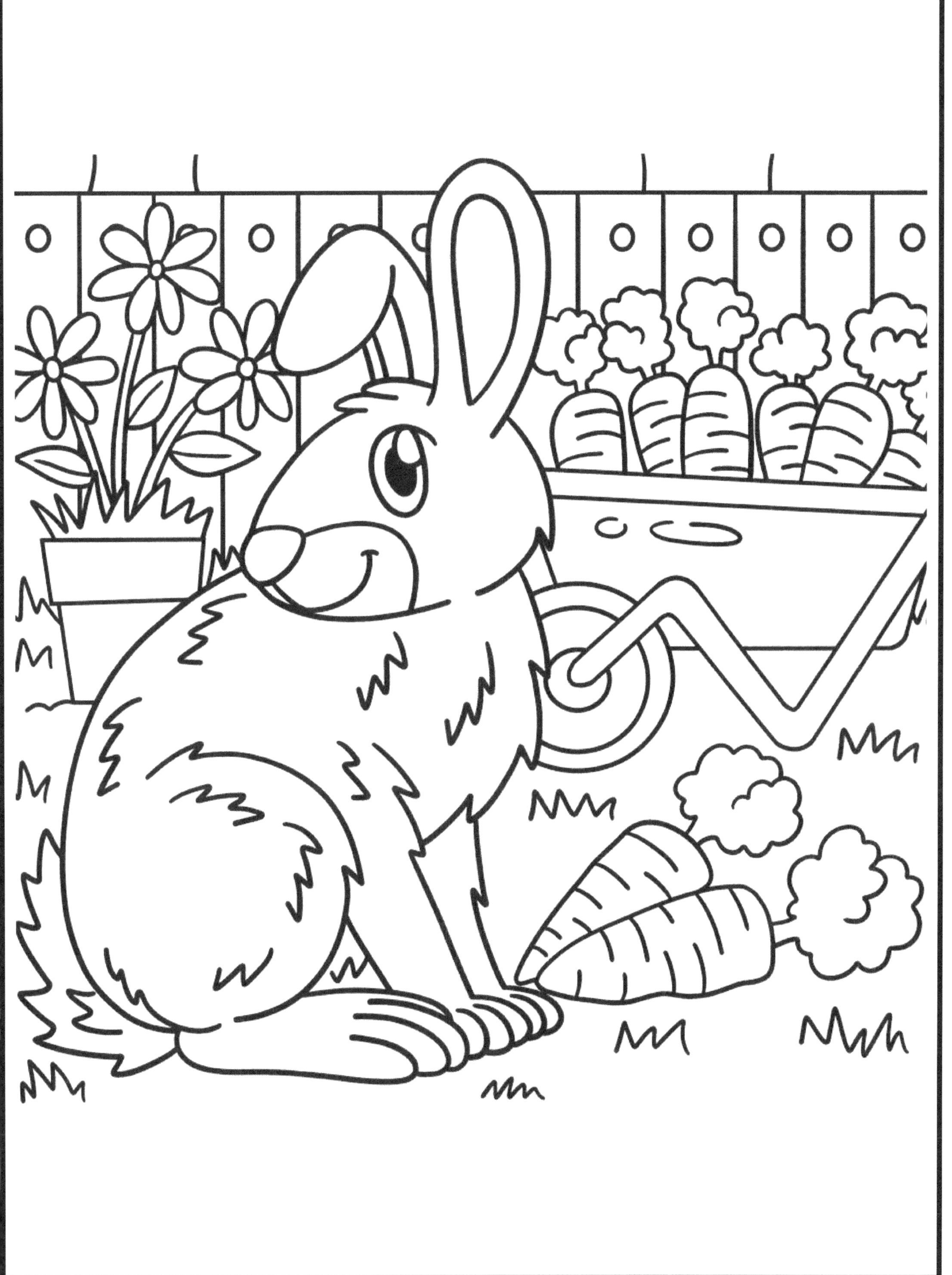

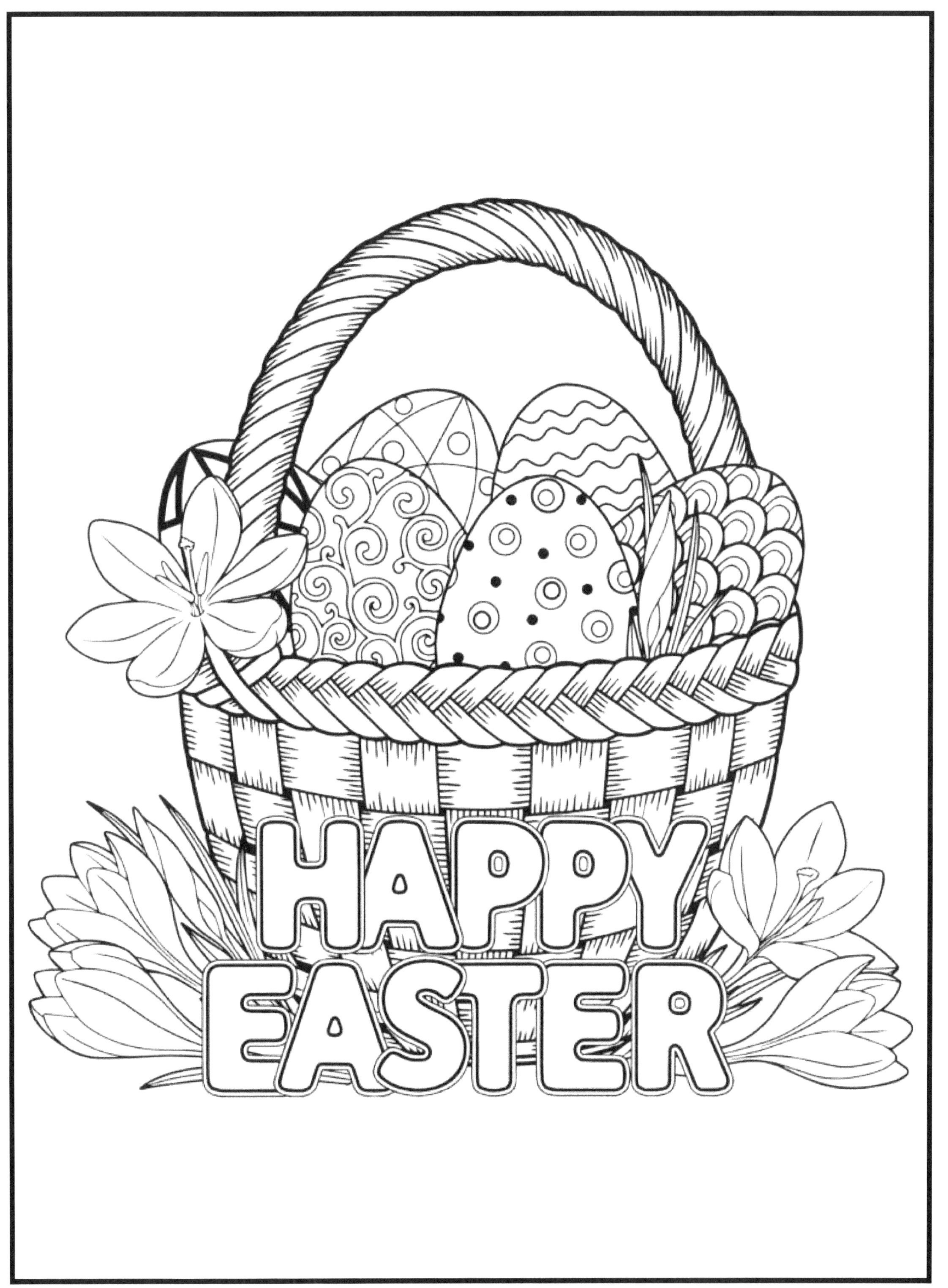

HAPPY
EASTER

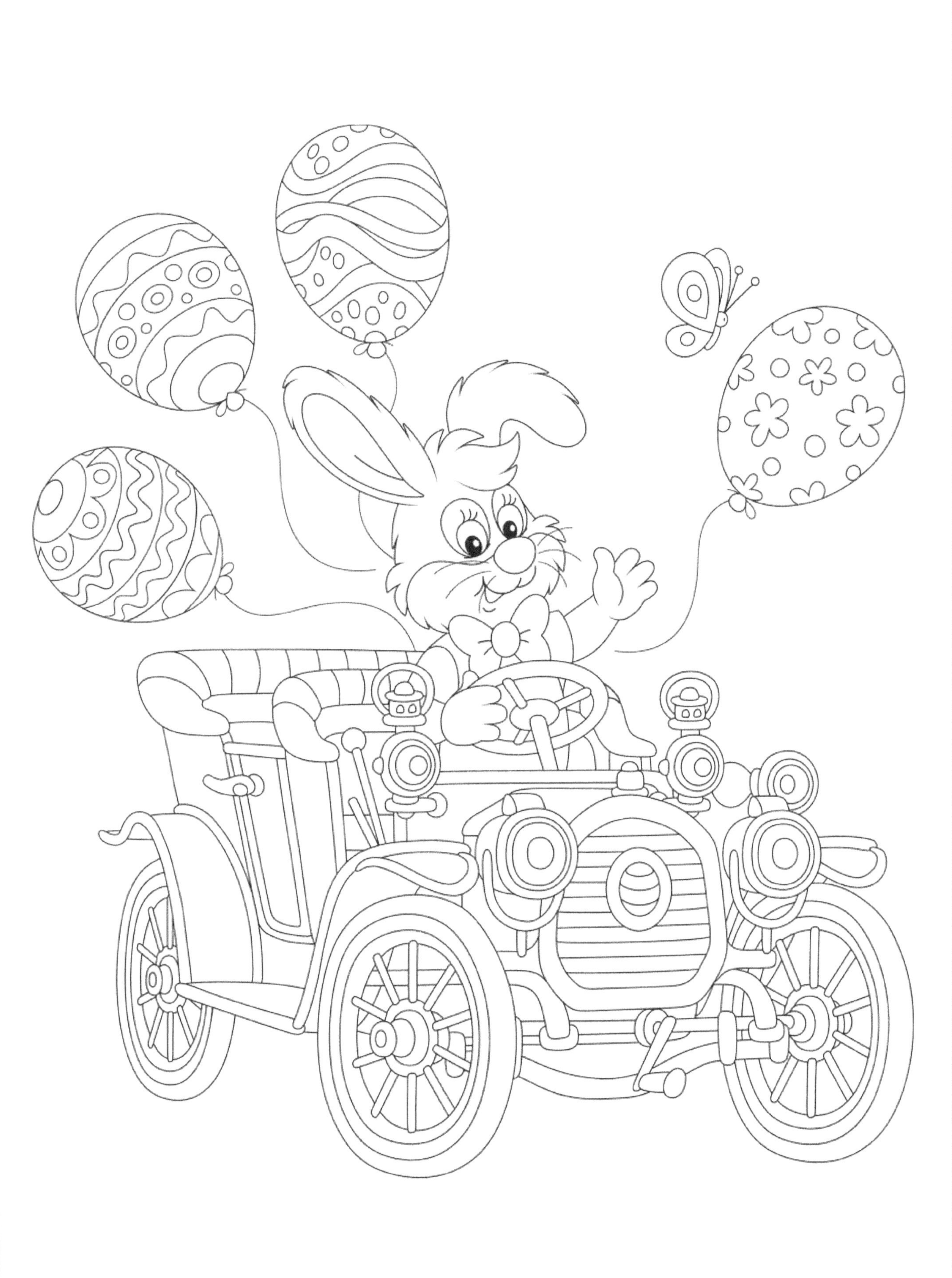

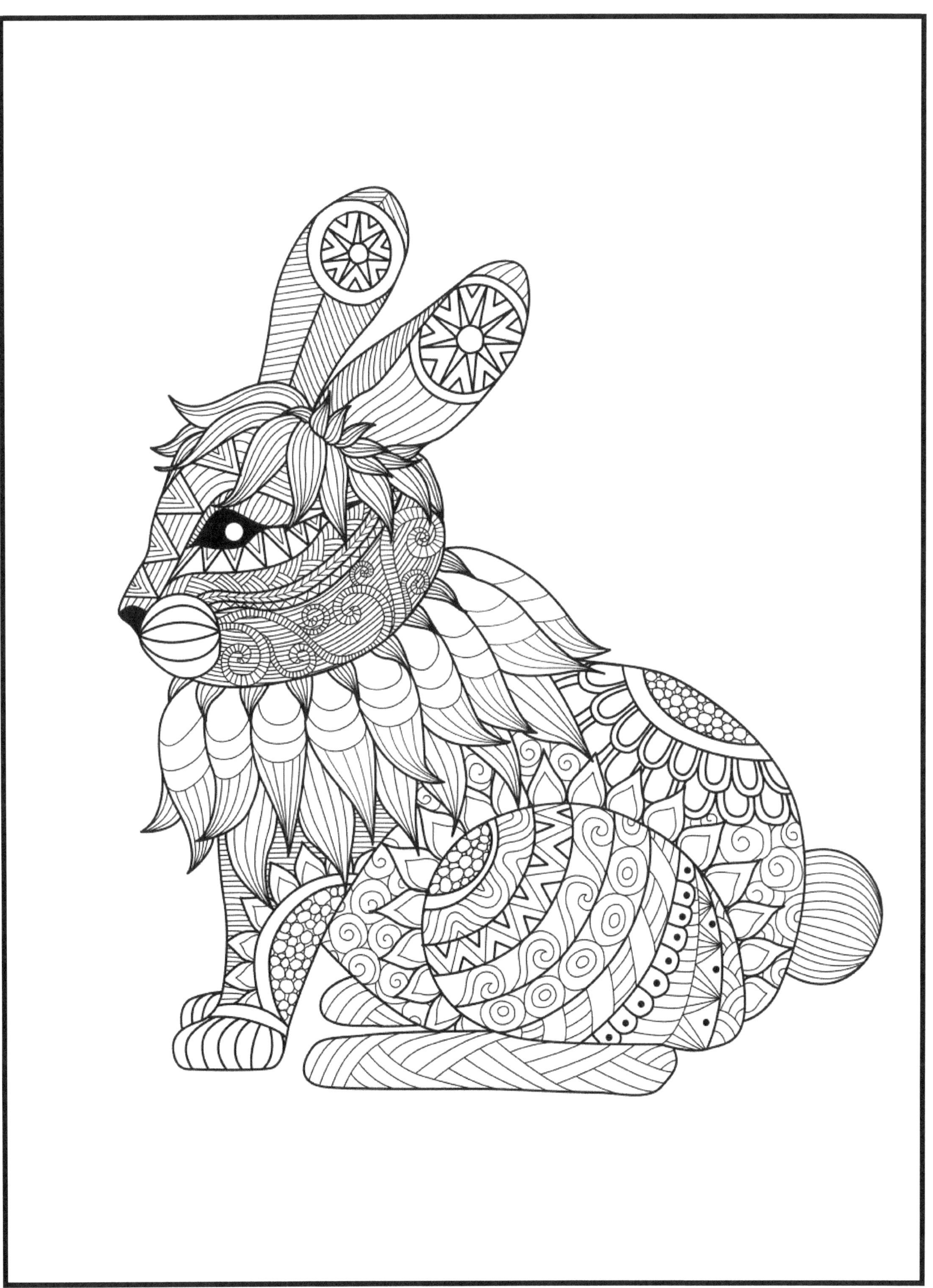

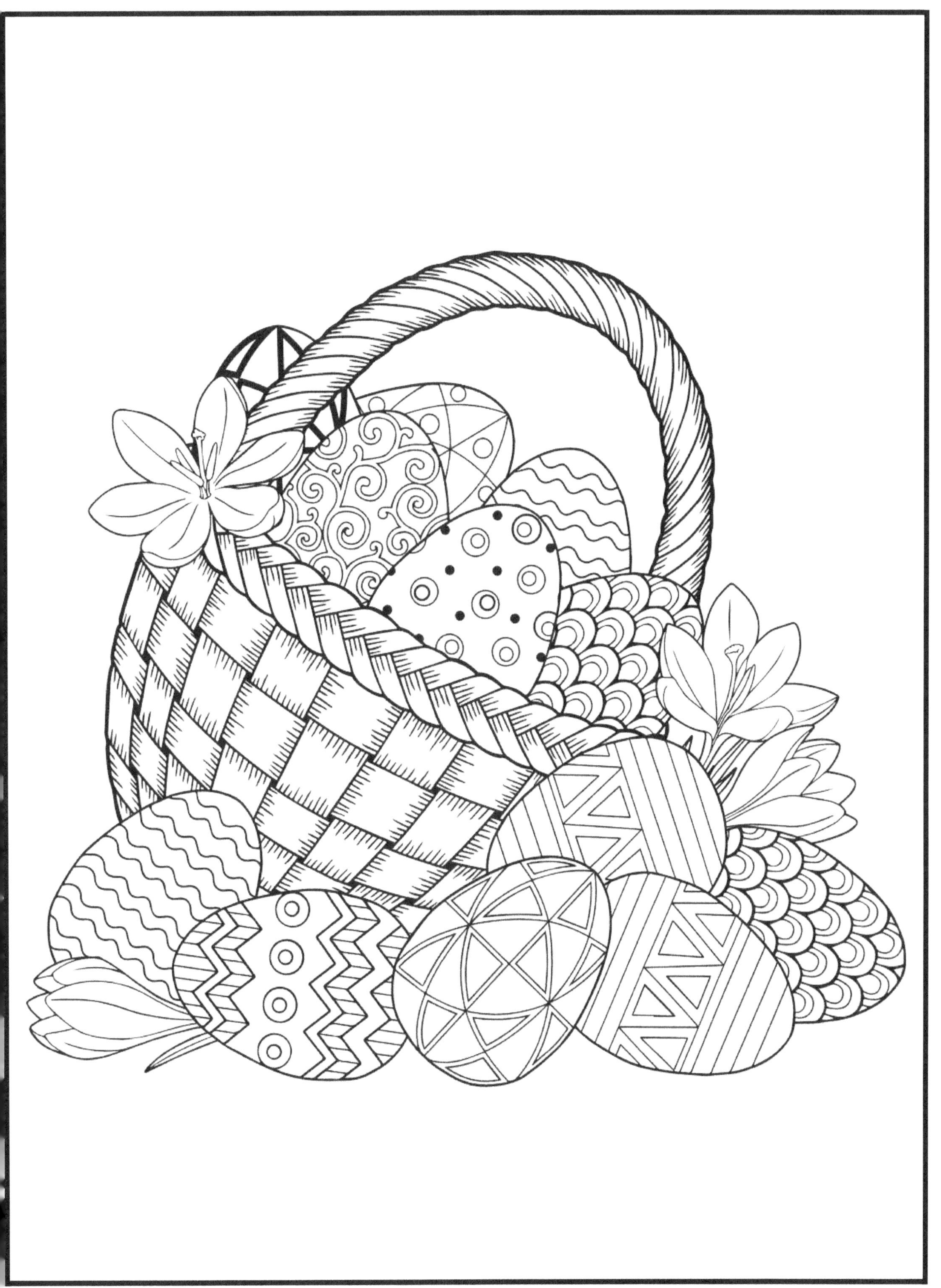

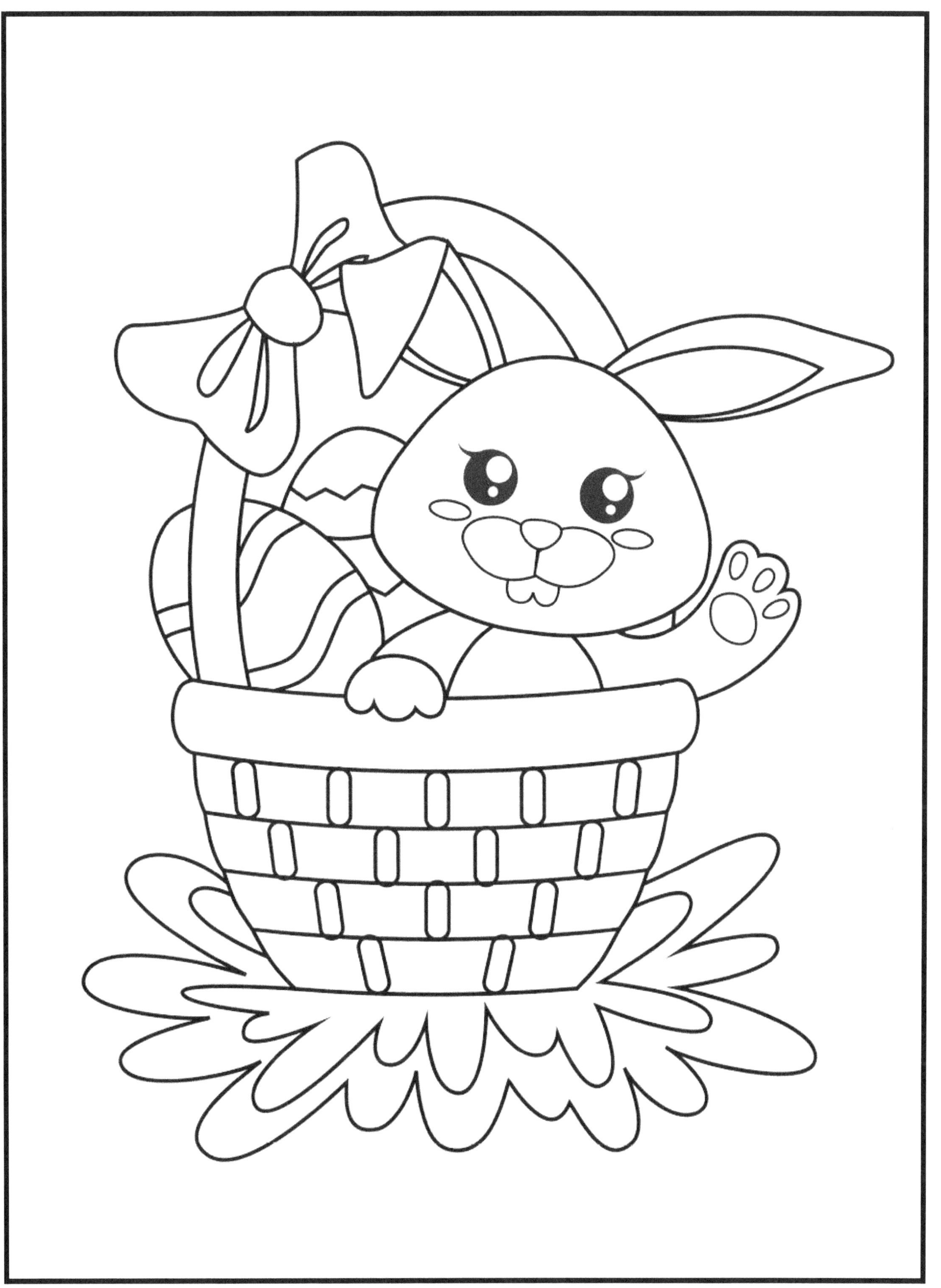

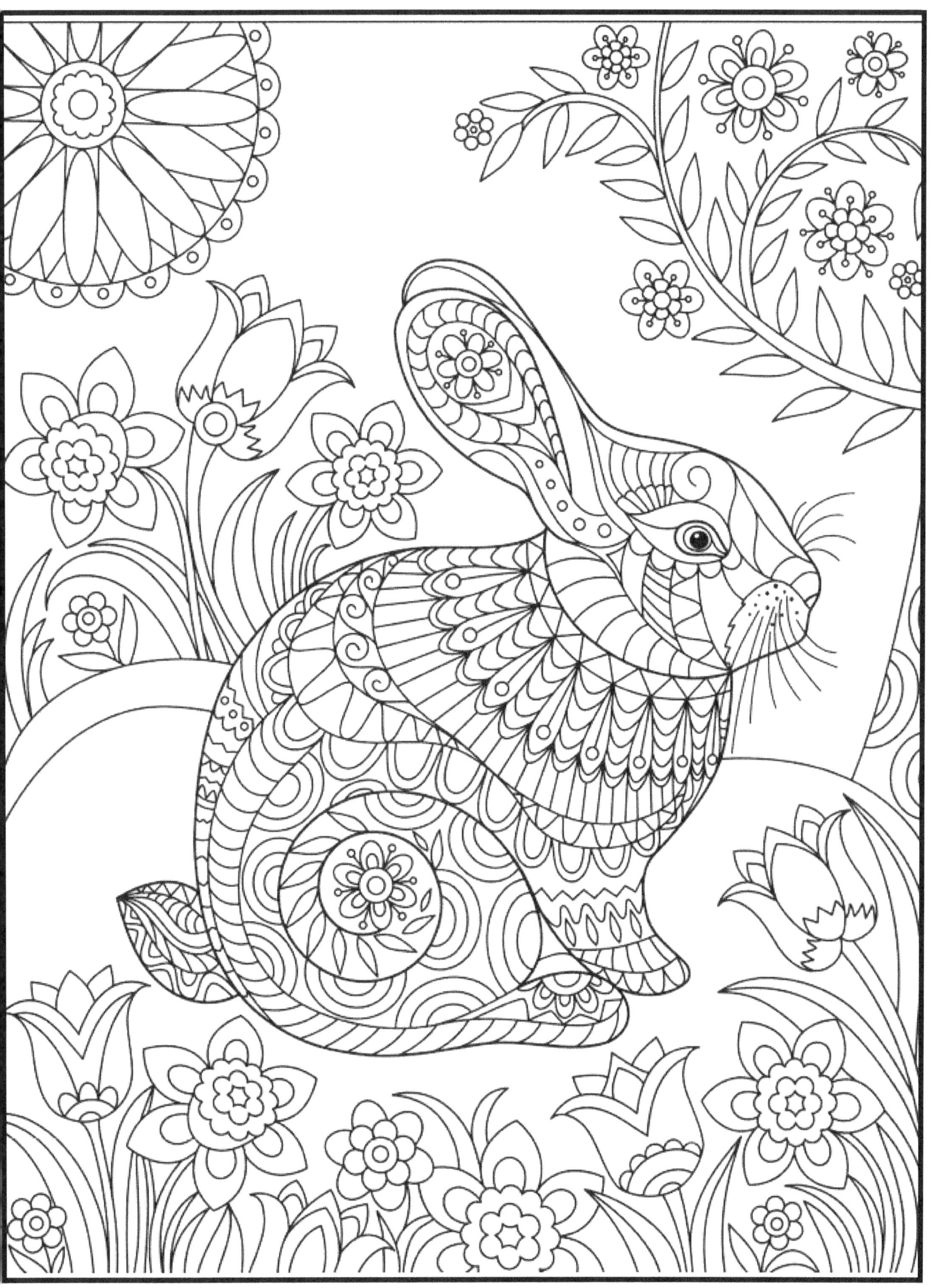

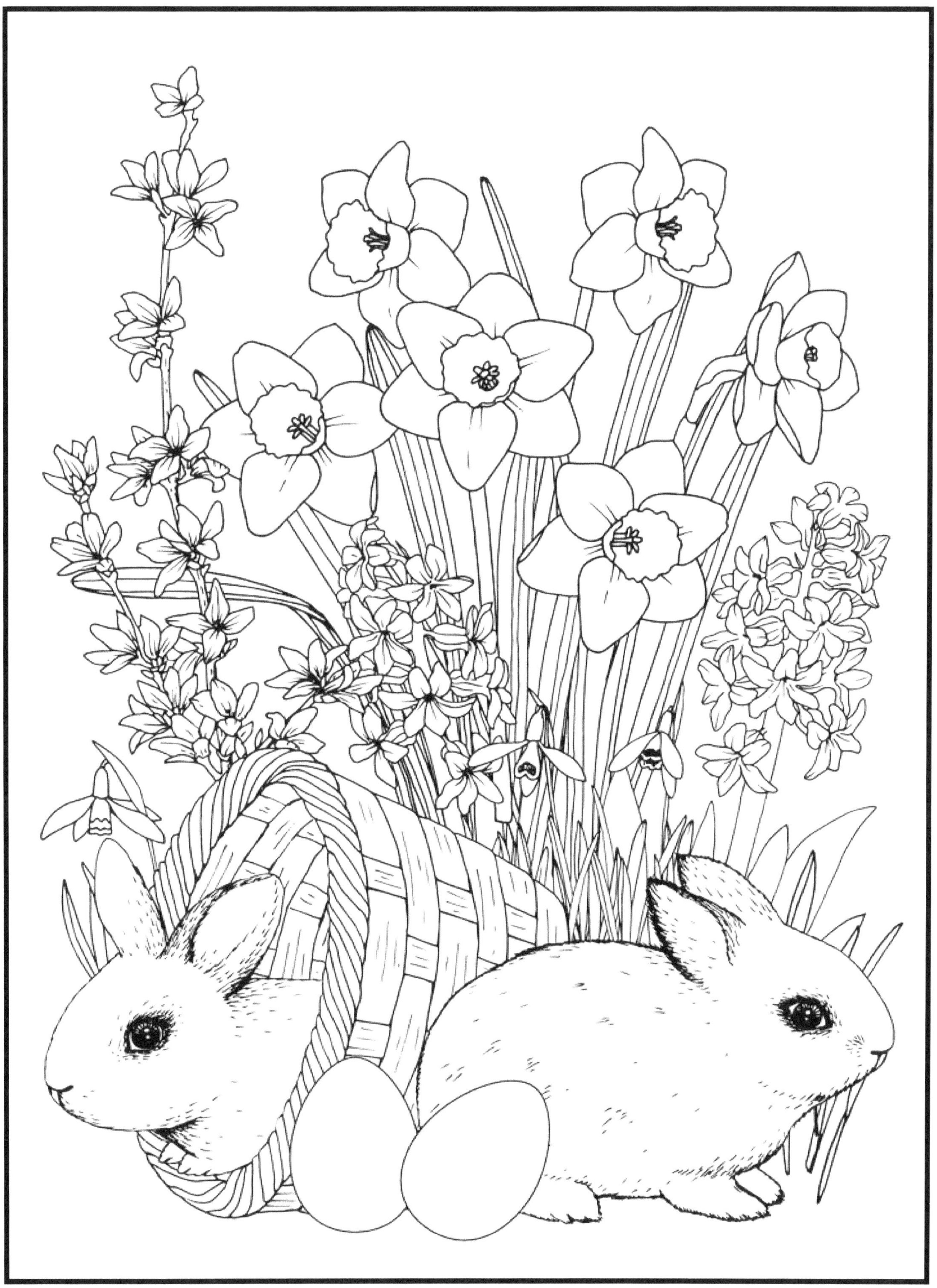

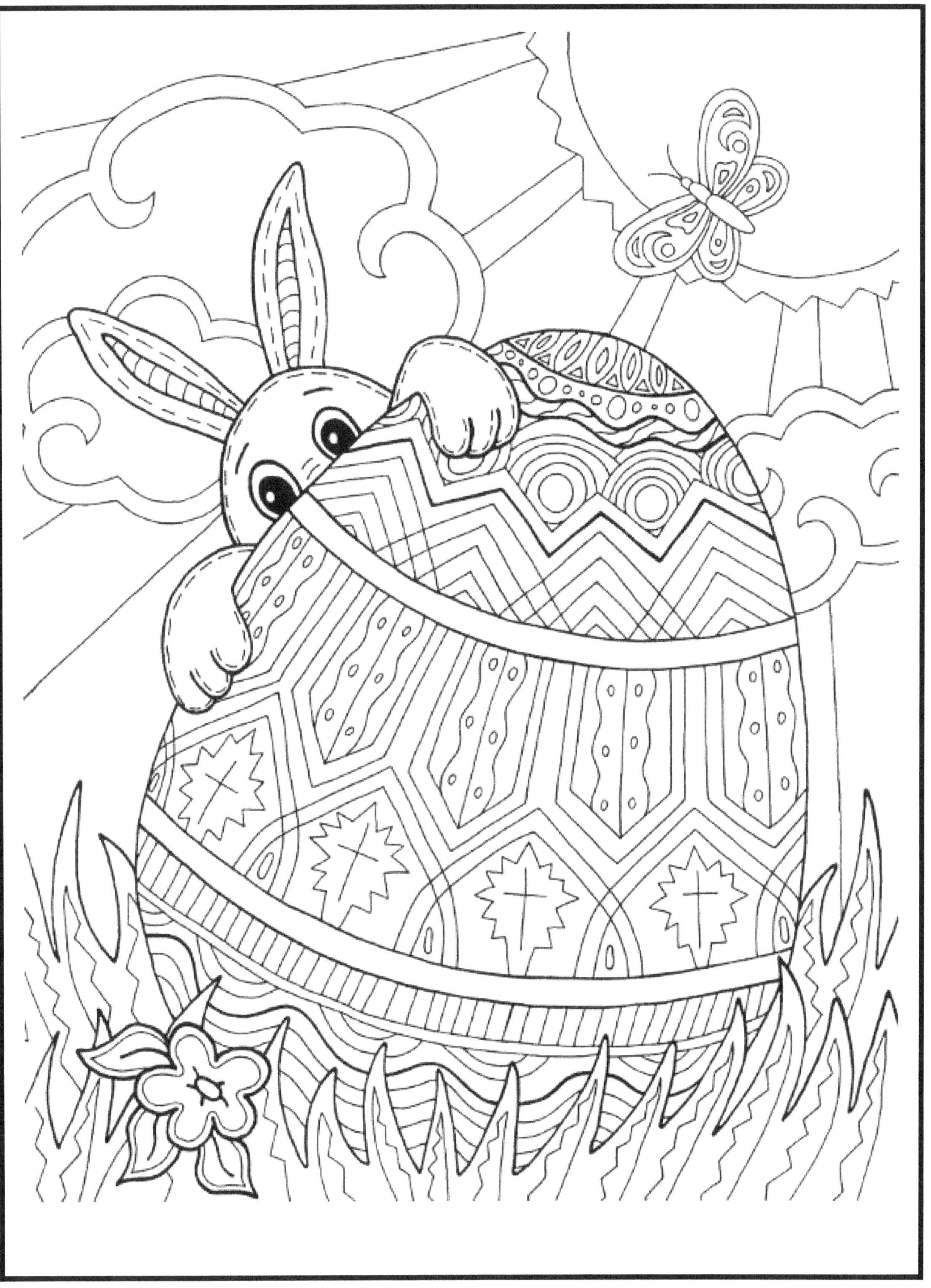

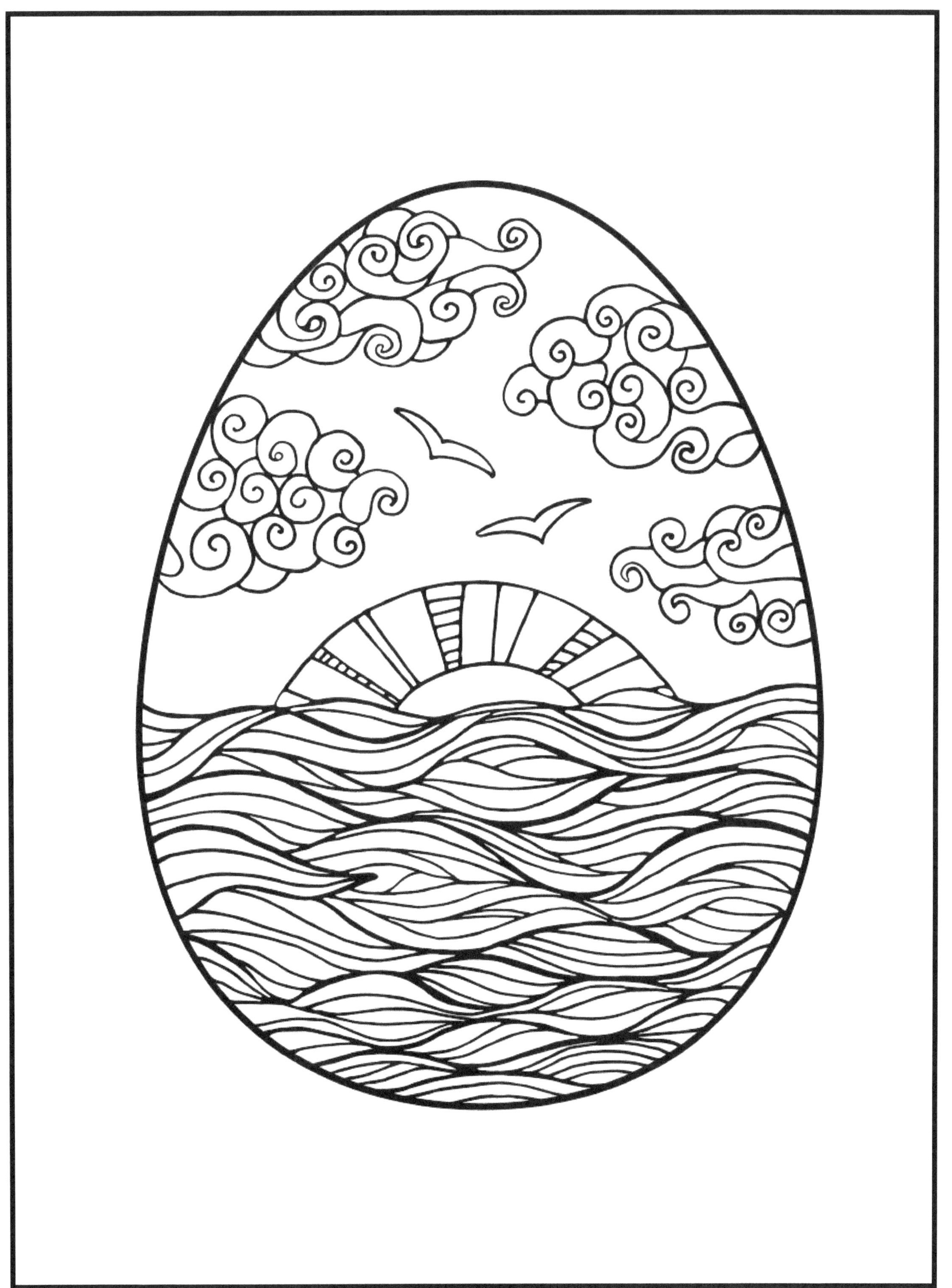

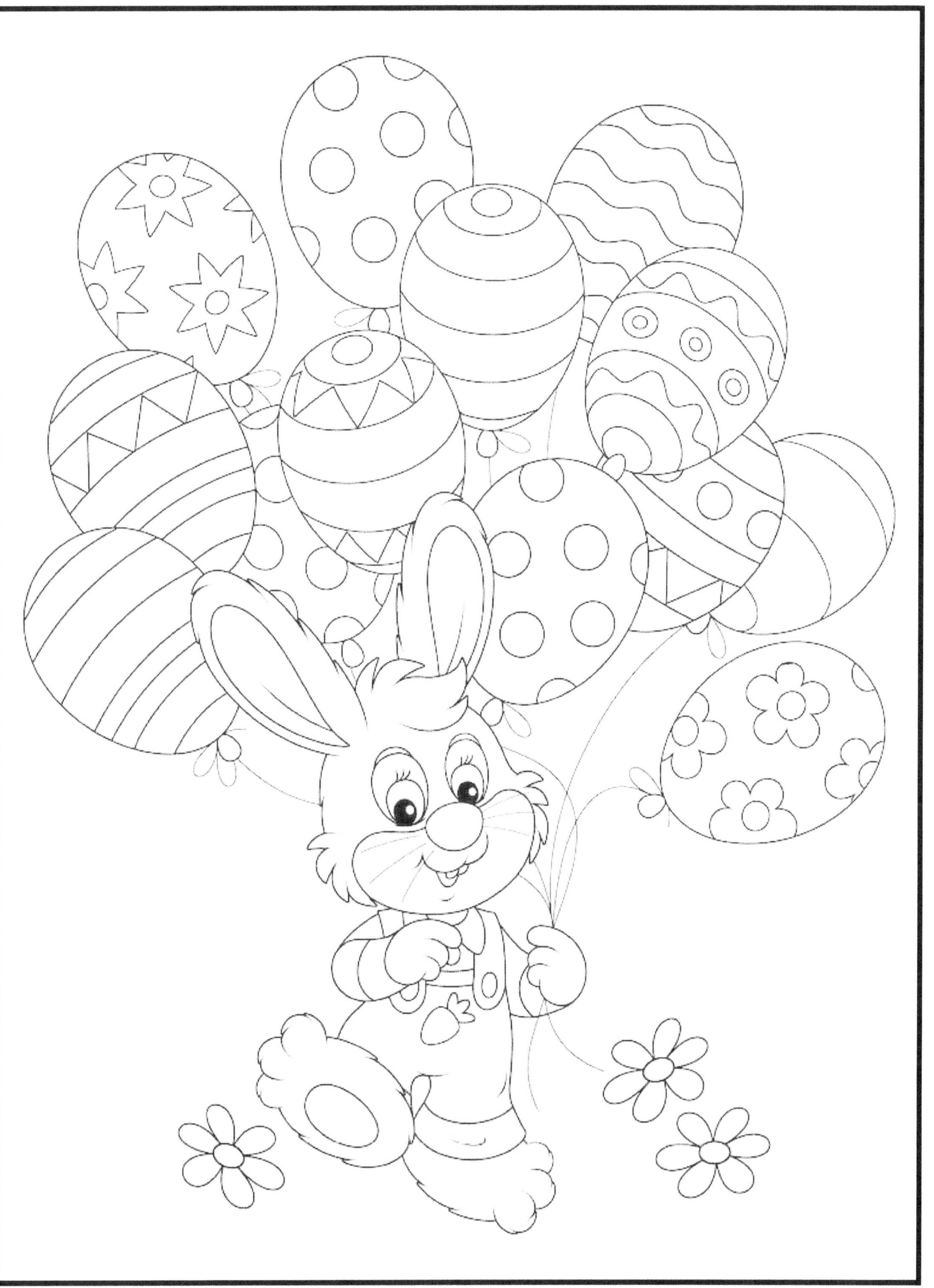

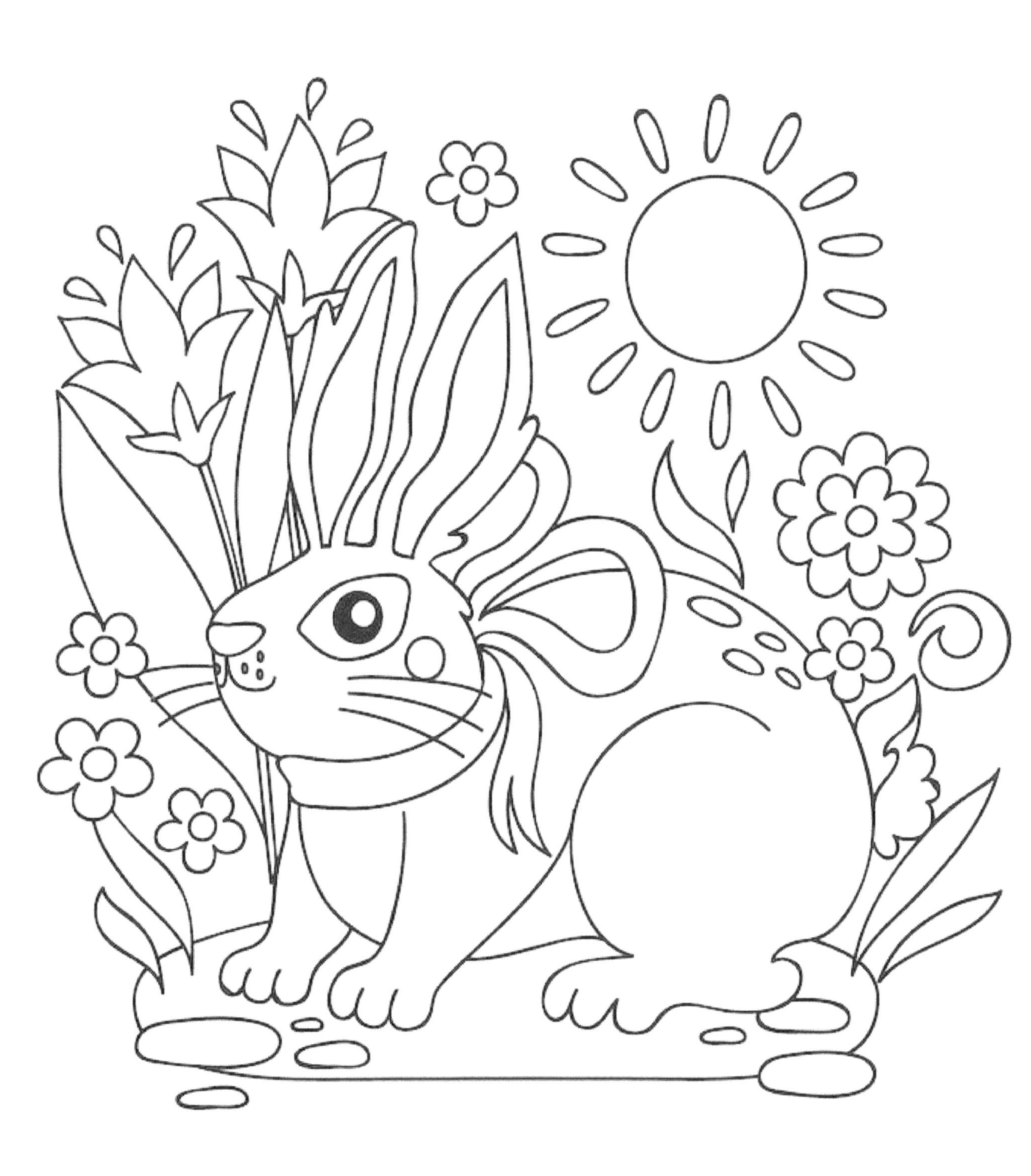

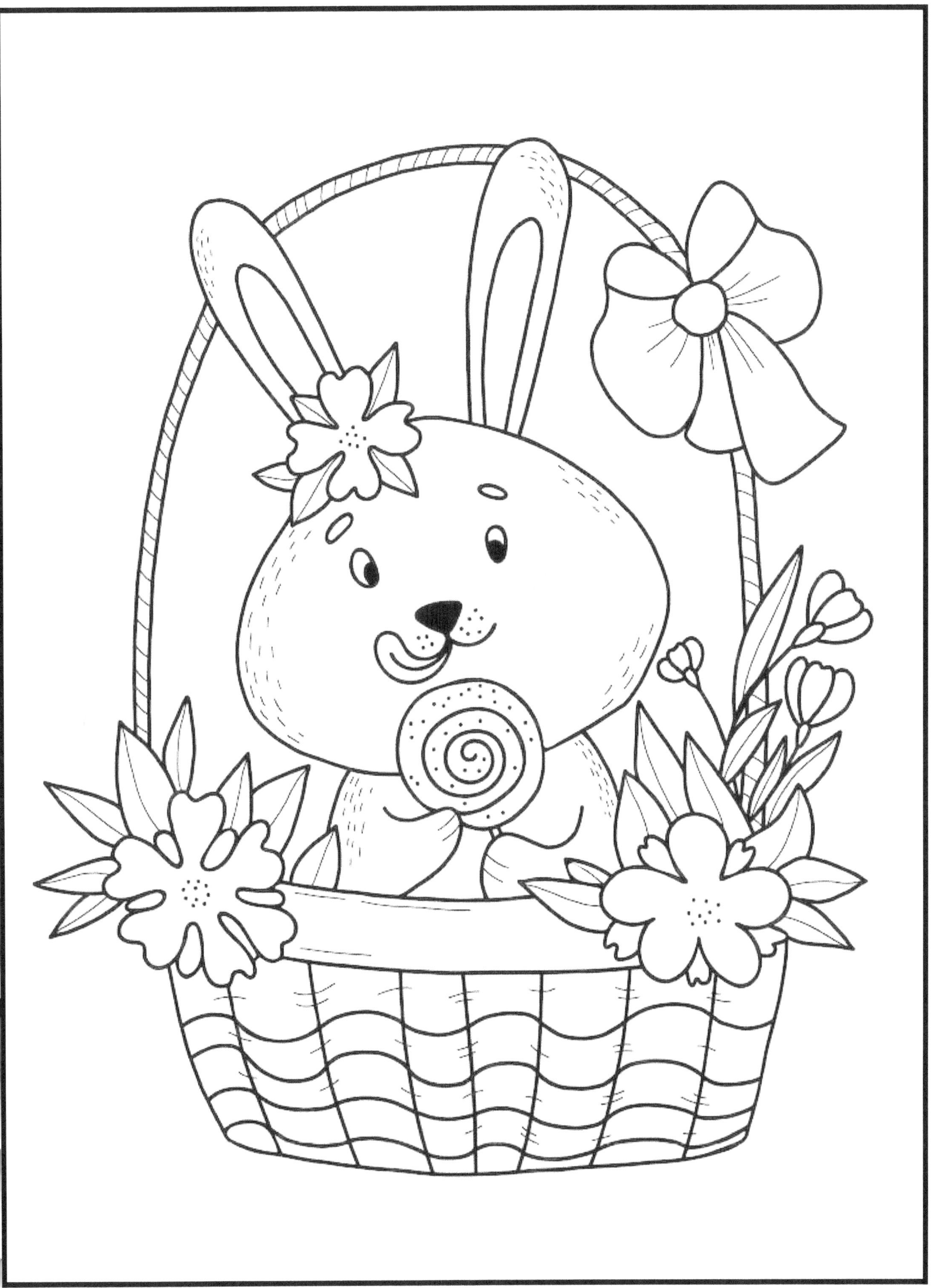

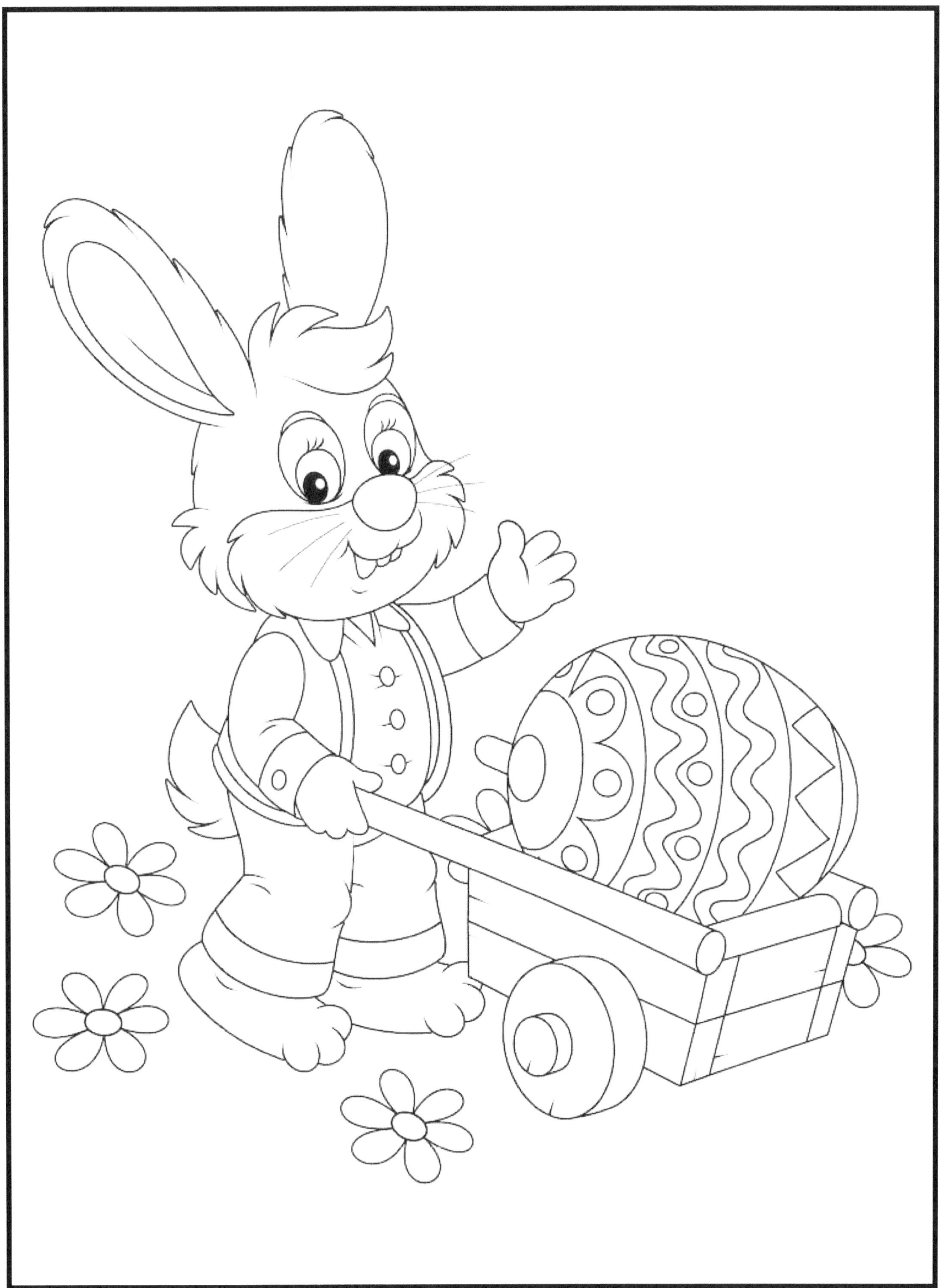

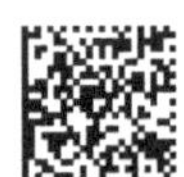